Tasting Success

Your Guide to Becoming a Professional Chef

Charles M. Carroll

WILEY

John Wiley & Sons, Inc.

Photos were taken by the author unless otherwise noted.

This book is printed on acid-free paper. ∞

Copyright © 2011 by John Wiley & Sons, Inc. All rights reserved.

Published by John Wiley & Sons, Inc., Hoboken, New Jersey.
Published simultaneously in Canada.

Library of Congress Cataloging-in-Publication Data:

Carroll, Charles M., 1964-
  Tasting success: Your guide to becoming a professional chef/Charles Carroll.
    p. cm.
  Includes index.
  Summary: "This book identifies the challenges that individuals would face
when starting down the road to become a chef and outlines the right paths to take.
It explores everything from family values, discipline, and how to acquire integrity, to
focus, charisma, commitment, and initiative. Cooks and chefs will also find out what
they need to do to excel in the classroom all the way to building their first team as an
executive chef."—Provided by publisher.
  ISBN: 978-0-470-58154-4 (hardback: acid-free paper)
  1. Food service—Vocational guidance—United States. 2. Cookery—Vocational
guidance—United States. 3. Cooks—Training of—United States. I. Title.

  TX911.3.V62C395 2011

  647.95023—dc22

                                                                2010022376

Printed in the United States of America

10 9 8 7 6 5 4 3 2 1

I would like to dedicate this book to
"My Three Girls"
Kelsey, Randi, and Torill.

Thank you for all of your love, patience, and understanding.

Contents

Foreword

Sometimes something just happens that takes you out of your normal thinking zone. You get one of those breakthrough "what *if*" kind of thoughts. I had one the other day riding my bike along the ocean, listening to music. The song was "Gimme Shelter" and when it ended I thought, "What if The Rolling Stones *didn't* have over 40 years of great hits but only one?"

What if "Gimme Shelter" was simply *if?* No "Satisfaction," "Jumping Jack Flash," "Beast of Burden," or any number of other classic songs. What if only one song made it on the charts from the one of the greatest rock and roll bands of all time?

Yet we can look at 'The Stones', as well as other (past and present) master artists, painters, playwrights, and truly take time to study them and the evolution of their work. But, sometimes, life is such that you don't get the benefit of the songs, paintings, influences of acknowledged "masters." What then?

Always remember that *one* person can come by *one* single day, *one* hour of *one* afternoon, or maybe it is *one* job you hold down for a period of time, or *one* amazing book. And, if you are *not* listening, *not* paying attention, *not* tasting, or worse, thinking that something truly valuable *could not come* from this person, you can miss "the lesson." To miss that valuable lesson is even sadder than being a "one hit wonder."

In Chef Charles Carroll's inspirational new book *Tasting Success: Your Guide To Becoming a Professional Chef,* you'll find a treasure trove of lessons he has gathered throughout his life and because of his dedication to the culinary arts, as well as lessons from several "masters" from other walks of life. There is no doubt we will learn from them . . . but Chef Carroll also tells us that aside from these "masters," someone, *and you never know who that someone may be,* can come into your life and teach you something that just might help you "work like a champion" and even possibly "become a master."

I have a life full of people who have taught me lessons that have shaped the chef I am today.

One of the many chefs who gave me an important lesson one snowy afternoon in Greeley, Colorado, has lasted me a lifetime of cooking. His name was Fred Boomer. He cooked in the U.S. Navy and then, after his discharge, got jobs along the way in all kinds of places. I met him when I scored a much-needed job as a cook in the Holiday Inn of Greeley. Yes, you read that right. I, and many other chefs, had their beginnings in ordinary places . . . working with chefs with no more formal training or "rock star" elements than cigarette-smoking, whiskey-drinking, pompadour-coiffed, redheaded Chef Fred. He gave me some advice about making soup that day (and he was none too happy with the question I asked that started the lesson) and I've never forgotten it. His teaching prepared me to make a soup *correctly* and, for the first time, I understood a glimmer of *why* it worked. It was about cooking *in a sequence* to create "layers of flavors." His jargon was not so clear but a spoonful of that soup expressed it fully. I read a similar lesson in the renowned cookbook author Paula Wolfert's seminal work, *The Cooking of Southwest France,* ten years later when I was teaching a young man named Charlie Trotter about sauce-making. In her book, the technique was called "stratification." Read it. I did, and Charlie Trotter did too.

I worked another job in Key West many years ago, for an African-American man named "Sammy," at an all-night barbeque joint. One day early on he scowled at me through thick black-framed glasses and leaned his aging but still fighting-trim body into me and said, "You ain't ready! You ain't got a *prep* list made up!" And he was right. He taught me that I wasn't *set up for success.* I worked there only six months, but walked away with a lesson that lasts me to this day: *Make a prep list.* If you want to be successful, you need to be *set up* for success.

I looked all around me during my first ten years of cooking. I worked with men and women on those hot lines who were often two to three times older than me. Most were still working for an hourly wage. Some of them lived in boarding houses or trailers. Some had no family. Yet they all taught me lessons with their lives. Sometimes it was one lesson per chef, fellow line cook, or dishwasher. (Don't rule out learning from anyone.)

So pay attention. "Mastery" doesn't get handed to you as you cross the stage on your Graduation Day. You might think so. Your parents might *hope* so. It has only just begun. But it has begun! I can honestly say that after all these years I love cuisine, cooking, growing, and doing it with my peers and family because it keeps opening up, inspiring, feeding me—intellectually, physically, and emotionally—and feeding those I love. *Tasting Success* can be as important to you and your success as your knife bag. But it won't do you any good any more than that knife bag unless you open it up and use it.

—*Chef Norman Van Aken*

Preface

Raise Your Hand If You Want to Fail

Who wants to fail? . . . Anyone? . . . Please stand up and be accounted for!

Some industry publications have reported that within ten years only 13 percent of that year's hospitality graduates would still be in the hospitality business. That statistic alone should be enough to concern anyone thinking about entering the culinary or hospitality field.

This statistic can change, and the reason I wrote this book is simple: I care about people entering the culinary field. I care about the road they choose to take. Over the past few years, I have experienced new culinarians entering the field with the attitude "I need it right now, give it to me so I can move on." That is what concerns me about the future of the industry. Among young culinarians today, there seems to be a lack of commitment and willingness to take the necessary time to see things through. This, I believe, is the result of many things, including the rise of the celebrity chef and the plethora of cooking reality television shows, coupled with the fact that young people are growing up in a digital world where everything moves at warp speed. The goal of this book is to help those getting started in the industry—whether just entering school or at their first kitchen job—make the right decisions in today's world, decisions that will steer them toward success. I outline what I believe to be the most important, tangible things one can do to achieve—to taste, if you will—the success desired. I also want to inspire chefs who work with these young professionals.

The Goals of This Book

This book is for every student in the beginning months of their education, or every new employee just starting out in a new hospitality job. It will be a home run in any introductory course for the culinary, foodservice, or hospitality industry, as well as a boon for career-planning or career development courses, intern- or externships, leadership and organizational development classes, or self study. In my opinion, it should be made available to all students with their knives and uniforms, for the simple reason that it will help them plan their success, plan their time, and research their future while they are in school. This book coaches students how to attack their time and plan their future.

I am here to say that you can be successful and you can be happy. I pride myself in aiding and mentoring new professionals in the culinary field to be successful. In fact, I have two programs within my property that provide a training ground for those new professionals who wish to "*chew off the end of the table to be successful!*" I love that. You will hear me repeat that several times throughout this book. I am very proud of the environment I provide and continue to develop for my culinary staff, and of those who have benefited from it. They are culinarians who do whatever it takes to be successful, who chewed off the ends of tables to be successful. These are the individuals I will go to bat for 100 percent of the time.

I thrive on team building and helping new professionals be successful. I take very seriously mentoring them into their first job with a great salary and great benefits and privileges. To me, that feels great! And when I get those "thank you" phone calls from past employees, I could not be any prouder. Whether they need advice or just want to talk about their success, I love every minute of it.

Does anyone really want to fail? It seems to me, nobody wakes up in the morning and says, "I feel good today, I think I want to fail." Truth be told, I am sure if you polled one thousand people and asked them if they want to be successful in life and in their career, 99.99 percent would tell you that they do. I have had the great pleasure of speaking to thousands of culinary students over the past several years. Many times I ask the question, "Who wants to be successful?" and once in a blue moon I get a student who wants to be that one person who is not afraid of being different, who will stand up and say, "I don't need to be successful, I just need to be happy."

I admire these people—to a point. Everybody wants to be happy. I would love to be happy every minute of every day, but the truth of the matter is that this may not always be possible. Furthermore, chances are if you are not successful in whatever you desire to be or do, you probably will not be happy.

Where are You Going, What are You Doing, and How are You Going to Get There?

If you are reading this book, you are linked to the hospitality field in one way or the other, or are about to become a culinary student in one of the many great culinary schools in the world. I applaud your enthusiasm and I am here to help you be successful. I will share with you lessons I have learned along the way as a member of seven U.S. Culinary Olympic Teams, the executive chef of three grand properties, a speaker at numerous culinary schools and organizations, and someone who enjoys just simply cooking at home.

From talking to many culinary students over the past several years, I realized that there is a need for a book like this that easily and clearly identifies the skills needed to be successful in your culinary career and explains how to master them. Moreover, in identifying these skills—including making a plan, effective time management, and researching opportunities—this book lays out the various ways to incorporate them into your daily schedule and create positive and effective work habits. Creating positive work habits is the first step on your journey to success. Failure, financing, and time management seem to be the top concerns of students of today. Lack of a plan is the first culprit of much of the failure in our industry. It astounds me that many students do not think past culinary school graduation. If there is no thought toward a post-school path, that means nothing has been done to prepare for the future, let alone the first job. It is difficult to succeed in anything if you don't have a plan.

Who is this book for? It is for any cook or chef, potential chef or cook—or any professional, for that matter—who wants to be successful. This book is for any person looking for a recipe for success and searching for the best road to take. This book identifies the challenges and hurdles that culinarians, cooks, and chefs face in today's challenging world.

The tools that I put forward in this book will help you lay the foundation for your success. Each chapter includes:

- Great lessons and life stories from champions in the culinary world, the world of sports, and the world stage
- A summary of chapter lessons
- A Game Plan to put the tools discussed within each chapter into action

Many chapters also include words of wisdom from leading educators across the United States as well as motivational quotes from culinary figures and other well-known people.

Great success does not happen to people unwilling to put the time and work into it. This book discusses the challenges in today's market, such as how to work hard, how to find the right opportunities, how to find the right mentor, how to work successfully, how to be successful, and how to find the time to be great. We will talk about values, self-discipline, acquiring and maintaining integrity, focus, charisma, commitment, initiative, and much more. But none of this is worth the paper it's written on unless you believe in yourself. You must have the faith and discipline in your heart and the will to *want* to be great. My goal is to help pave that perfect road that will lead you toward your success; ultimately it will be up to you whether or not you decide to take the journey. Let's work together to achieve your success!

This book will not only prepare you for school, externship, work habits, and your first job, it will also enlighten you on just simply doing the right thing and growing into a great chef or manager. This is a great time in your life, and I want to help you with your personal success as I have done for thousands of other new professionals.

This is your time! The skills discussed in this book will aid in your success. Now let's get started. Let's start chewing those tables.

Acknowledgments

I would like to thank River Oaks Country Club, the Board of Directors, and Mr. Joe Bendy, General Manager, for their dedication and commitment to excellence and their constant support of my culinary team.

Thank you to all the champions I had the great pleasure to meet and interview for this book. Not only do they add amazing life lessons and inspiration to the book, but they were a true inspiration to me. I was incredibly humbled to be in their presence and have learned a great deal from their generosity and true-to-heart kindness. They are real champions in all senses of the word.

To my entire culinary team at River Oaks Country Club for their loyal dedication and culinary passion. For constantly searching for their road to success and being courageous enough to go after it.

To Julie Kerr and Mary Cassells and the John Wiley family for continuing to believe in me.

To all the new friends and professionals who have read *Leadership Lessons from a Chef: Finding Time to Be Great*, thank you for all your kind e-mails and words of encouragement. It means the world to me that my work has helped our culinary profession in some small way.

To Chef Norman Van Aken for taking time out of his crazy schedule to help me. A true gentleman and brilliant chef. He has been a great inspiration and a wonderful friend.

To John David Mann (best-selling author of *The Go-Giver*) for his wit, charm, and newly found interest in truffle oil. ☺

To my assistant Hilmi Ahmad for all her tireless patience and work dealing with me, organizing my office, and making this project a truckload easier. I throw all the balls in the air, and she has a magical way of first juggling them, and then catching each of them one at a time.

Introduction: What's Your Plan?

There's No Substitute for Experience

Lack of a Plan

I wish I had a dime for every time I have asked a student what he or she wanted to do after graduation and received the answer, "Get a good job somewhere, hopefully." What kind of success is this person going to have with an answer like that? A lot of money is being or has been spent on your education. Why would you leave it up to chance as to where you get a job and what direction your career takes you?

In my opinion, the **lack of a plan** is the number one reason culinary students and professionals fail, quit, or decide to leave the hospitality sector and change fields. It's up to you to create and execute a plan for what you want to do, what your goals are, and how you will achieve success. If you have no idea where you want to go, how will you know when you get there?

> If you have no idea what you are doing, where you are going, or how you're going to get there, you will probably fail.

Too many times I have been told by students that they have no idea what they want to do after graduation. It's OK not to have all the answers—nor are you expected to—but if you're not directing your energy to finding some of the answers, you will probably end up in the statistical pile of culinary failures. Consider the following scenario:

You have graduated from culinary school with a degree and have landed a good job with a property that has a great reputation. While in school, you really did not think much about which part of the industry you like the best; you just wanted to land a good job. You start out as a line cook making twelve dollars an hour. You are a good employee, always on time, always do what you are told, and get along with everyone. After the first year, you receive a 3 percent raise; the second year, you receive another 3 percent raise. After two years, everyone loves you and you can work any station on the line. After the third year, you receive yet another 3 percent raise, and now you are making almost thirteen dollars an hour. This is just one dollar more than you made when you started the job three years ago. You realize you can't pay the bills, you can't live on this ridiculous salary, and you certainly cannot pay back your school loans. How the heck are you supposed to make it?

What did you do wrong? You deserve more, right? You did well in school, got great grades, did whatever anybody asked you to do at work—so where is the money? You've been doing great work, so why is no one jumping through hoops to move you to the next level? After all, the culinary field is glamorous, with celebrity rock star chefs, culinary reality shows, and iron chef competitions. You are entitled to do great, to make great money and be successful, right? Instead, you are thinking about quitting because you cannot afford to be a chef.

Heck, you can dig ditches for the city and get paid sixteen dollars an hour and get all holidays and weekends off. Ladies and gentlemen, in my humble opinion, this is the number one reason recent graduates from the hospitality field quit. *THERE WAS NO PLAN!* That is the purpose behind the strategies in this book. If you use this book as the "bible of your work ethic," and you stick to many of the exercises in this book, you will be on the road toward success. Simply reading it will not make you successful; you have to do the exercises. Buying a computer does not make you more efficient, organized or smarter, but using it to its full potential may.

Climbing the Ladder

What are your expectations? Do you expect to get everything for nothing? Receive all the bonuses without the hard work? Receive all the great jobs with no real background? Receive a big salary just because you have a diploma? In other words, do you feel entitled and expect to receive what you want, when you want it, without having to work for it? Or are you willing to work hard to climb the ladder one rung at a time, just as everyone before you had to do? Climbing the ladder is much, much harder, requires much more energy and time. But it is the only way you will truly receive success and reach whatever height you determine you want and are willing to work for.

So, rule number one:

There is NO substitute for experience.

NONE! So forget about skipping the part about gaining experience. Yes, you may spend several years working every station in the kitchen, but that's the price you pay for experience. But what's your plan to go forward? You must have a plan, because it is unlikely anyone else will make the effort to move you forward and upward if you don't indicate that's what you want to happen. Nor can you trade grades for experience or get credit in your workplace because you did well in school. You cannot download, burn, bum, beg, borrow, or steal experience. I can tell you dozens of stories of graduates who worked ten months at a property and figured they had the system down and were ready for the executive chef's job.

Experience is the cornerstone to your foundation and will dictate how big and strong your house will be. Your success will be based on your track record and your experience. I am going to help you with this concept throughout the book, but for now, please understand that your value and success will be judged and weighed on your past experiences, on where you have worked and for whom you have worked. If you can't back up your track record with skill, if you don't have a great foundation of cooking and experience, you will be quickly found out. Your subordinates will find the holes in your foundation, and your house will come down. Your reputation and track record are vitally important to your success.

> Your success will be based on your track record and your experience.

It's important for you to be incredibly eager, yet humble. "Humble" is a delightful word. What does it mean, really?

Humble: Not proud or haughty; not arrogant or assertive; ranking low in a hierarchy or scale.

Humility is one of the toughest and biggest lessons for students and young culinarians to learn. I remember when I was just starting out and I was so eager to climb the ladder, I oftentimes overlooked the basics. At the same time, my commitment and my dedication overshadowed many of my failures, due to the fact that I just wanted success so badly. I was willing to do whatever it took to be successful. I would listen to any chefs who would give me guidance, and I trusted their judgment.

The Plan

This whole book is about *your plan.* Everything in this book will help you with your road map to success, but to get started, I want you to think about this exercise and use the tools discussed throughout the book to formulate your plan going forward. Here are the first couple of steps in formulating your plan.

Step One: First you need to figure out what it is you want to do. Are you going to culinary school to be a chef? One great thing you have going for you is that you know you love to cook. What I want to challenge you to do now is to determine what kind of cook you want to be. What field within the culinary world do you want to work in? Fine dining venues, resorts, hotels, freestanding restaurants, country clubs, and bakeries are just some of the options. You may not have the answer now, and that is OK. The most important thing is that you start thinking about it. Start asking questions. Ask your instructors what they think you would be good at. They may see qualities in you that you did not realize you possess. This exercise is a huge step in the development of your success. The sooner you have a feel for this, the quicker you can climb the ladder and home in on your goals. Don't wait until after graduation to find yourself saying, "I hope I can get a good job somewhere."

> Don't wait until after graduation to find yourself saying, "I hope I can get a good job somewhere."

Step Two: Research! When you have an idea of which field you want to be in, start learning as much as you can about it. You now have a place to start; you can now do research into the next layer of your road map to success. Research who the top four chefs in that area are, and in the areas of the country in which you are willing to work. You have the world at your fingertips.

The more you put into your research, the quicker you will grasp what it takes to be successful. Your focus will take on a whole new meaning, one with attention, a sense of urgency, desire, and understanding. We'll spend more time talking about these particular steps in your game plan in Chapters 5, 6, and 8.

Remember, you choose whether to be successful or not! Nobody else. If you choose to be successful, you will work hard and do whatever it takes to get there. If you choose not to work hard, chances are you will not be successful, or not as successful as you want to be.

> You choose whether to be successful or not!

Work Like a Champion

I have interviewed ten champions to provide ten illustrations of what it takes to be successful, to beat all odds and WIN, to achieve what so many people say that you can't achieve—and to ultimately work like a champion!

It was my privilege to speak with and to hear the stories of all the champions in this book. It has taught me a lot. It has helped me to further develop and respect who I want to be. It has shown me that, without a doubt, those who are focused, those who dream, those who never give up until they achieve, ultimately become successful. You may wonder: What does the heavyweight champion George Foreman have to do with my hospitality success? The truth of the matter is, in any successful person there are lessons that can be, and should be, learned. But what I want to amplify here is that in these stories you will hear a repeated theme, an attitude about how to be successful, and that attitude is:

Never give up until you achieve your goal.

It's as simple as that. Never give up! The difference between champions and the average Joe walking down the street is that the champions have heart, and they never gave up. Don't take their stories for granted or think they had things easy. Each and every one of them has had to work extremely hard to achieve his or her success. You can be the champion of your own dreams and goals. Read and understand their stories, really understand what they went through. The more you learn about others' successes, the more educated you will be on preparing yourself and doing the right thing.

Once you understand that the biggest secret is never to give up, then the next big secret is to keep going, keep achieving, keep striving. What I have learned over the years is that when you achieve something great you feel great inside. But what has been a fantastic lesson is that, if you keep going, you'll find you can achieve ten times more. It is easy to say, "Yes, I did it," and put it away as a win. But instead, say, "OK, that was pretty cool, what else can I do?" or "How can I grow from here?" or "How can I make this current situation better?" It is not until that point, that epiphany, that you will ultimately see your true potential. So with that, let's get started and work like a champion.

Chapter Lessons

- First understand that there is no substitute for experience.
- Your success will be based on your track record and your experience.

- Be humble yet hungry.
- Develop your plan; study which avenue of the hospitality business you want to work in.
- Research the field you want to be a part of.
- Work like a champion!

Chapter 1

Stickability

Work Like a Champion

Researching and writing this book has been a fantastic experience. I have had the opportunity to interview famous chefs and others, all champions in their own area of expertise. I have been privileged to hear firsthand their stories of success, failure, and success again. Listening to them tell their stories so passionately made the hair stand up on the back of my neck. It made me dream about slipping into their shoes—not to be successful in their place, but to realize my own dreams. I want to do my best to share these champions' stories with you so that you can feel what I felt. I hope you all value the lessons from these champions.

Work Like a Champion and Stick to the Plan!

You may find it odd that I interviewed sports figures to be included in a book meant for inspiring, motivating, and helping new and future culinarians become successful in today's market. My reason is simple. I believe we all have to work like a champion, if we want to become a champion. We all have to have the heart of a champion, if we strive to be a champion. We all have to think the way a champion thinks, if we truly want to achieve our goals and aspirations of being champions. And, last but not least, we have to be dedicated and committed like a champion, or nothing will happen. You need "stickability," the willingness to stay your course and not give up at the first sign of trouble, to achieve the success you want.

> We all have to work like a champion, if we want to become a champion.

This is a very important point. You can't just "want." You can't just "hope." You can't just "dream." You have to *do* all of the above and then truly *believe*, in the deepest part of your heart, that you will achieve, that you will persevere no matter what. You will. It then becomes a matter of when, not if. When you read the stories of these champions, you will realize that they were not born champions; they worked hard for every bit of their success. Each survived several setbacks and failures before reaching success. You will realize that they never gave up! Period!

Never give up. Stick to your dreams. This is the chapter's—no, the book's—biggest message. The only difference between the champions in this book and the average person is that the champions worked and trained relentlessly until they achieved greatness.

> You have to be dedicated and committed like a champion, or nothing will happen.

After hearing everyone's stories, I realized there was one common thread connecting all the champions. No matter what kind of champion—sports star, celebrity chef, coach, or dean of culinary programs—one thing they all preach is the ability to "Stick To It!" I want to take a moment and drive this point home because I feel that many people, including me at different points in my life, believe that champions are untouchable. Being a champion, experiencing incredible success, and defying all odds are things that happen to other people, people on television. I am just a normal person, not a star; success at that level would never happen to me. Oftentimes we believe we can never be that champion. And with that attitude, you won't!

> All champions have one thing in common, the ability to Stick To It!

If there is one thing I have learned over the years, it is that all the people that I look up to, respect, and admire for their success in life—all of them, believe it or not—are real people. They sleep, eat, shower, and put their shoes on just like you and me. Becoming a champion is not easy; if it were, everyone would be a champion. Champions are special, few and far between. Being a champion takes courage and an uncompromising work ethic and dedication. Champions have the ability to get back up after they have been knocked down. They have the heart of a lion and the will of a warrior. There is no failure enormous enough to keep them down. But, in the end, they are real people. When you hear their stories, you will get a better understanding of what I am talking about.

> Champions have the heart of a lion and the will of a warrior.

I know everyone has heard this at one time or another. Your parents, teachers, and coaches have said it. But how many times have you actually taken that advice to heart? How many times have you dug that deep in your inner strength to succeed? Many people talk the talk, but in the end most would rather quit than work hard to achieve. It's more important to walk the walk. It is so much easier to quit than to work incredibly hard. Many individuals will quit when they reach their first obstacle. At the first sign of some form of resistance, they decide to quit because "it is just too hard." In reality, the problem is more likely a result of lost focus and laziness. Yet many of these individuals "wish" they were successful. Wish they were champions. Wish they made lots of money or were famous. Chef Norman Van Aken told me that an employee once asked him how to become famous. Is that the craziest thing you have ever heard?

I am a football fan and I love this quote I saw recently in the newspaper from San Francisco 49ers' head coach, Mike Singletary.

"I never considered myself a great player, I had just enough ability to be a good player, and I wanted to be a great player. The desire in me to work my tail off made it happen."

The goal here is to help you clearly define your work habits. I want to help you clearly define what kind of culinarian you want to be, and help you find the right road to get there. Most importantly, from reading all of my interviews with champions, I hope you clearly understand that the difference between champions and those who are not champions is simply that the champions never gave up. Never! They had a dream, they went after their dream, they worked through and learned from their failures and setbacks, they worked harder, and then they became champions. They stuck to it!

This is the point at which you must decide. You can either work like a champion and develop the work habits and work ethic of a champion, or you can wish you were a champion. You decide. You have to want it. I want you to want it so bad you can't stand it! I want you to want it so bad that you are willing to do whatever it takes to be successful. The secret is being true to yourself and sticking to it.

THE STORY OF STICKABILITY

As Told by Chef John Folse

This is a story attributed to Herman Perridan, an African-American restaurateur whose family used to operate a restaurant in the town of Opelousas, Louisiana. It's a very Cajun, French-oriented town. There are a lot of hardworking farmers and fishermen, and an abundance of farm country around that area. Herman married into a family that owned a local African-American restaurant, and they were famous for having only one item on the menu. Having only one item on a menu is contradictory to anybody's idea of success. That one item was duck. He had a duck restaurant during the 1950s, '60s and '70s, where all he served was roasted duck halves, with a multitude of fruit accompaniments.

John Folse

Having a single item on the menu in a restaurant run by an African-American family, in the middle of a Cajun town, a French–Acadian town, defied all odds of success. Yet, Herman Perridan found himself on the front page of *The New York Times* in an article that talked about a restaurant in the segregated South. I was just getting started as a young restaurateur and I was very interested in his success story. I decided if I was going to be successful, rather than re-invent the wheel, I needed to learn from the masters and their successes. Instantly my eyes turned to Perridan because he, against all odds, had not only been successful in Louisiana but also attracted a great white audience during a time of segregation.

I searched out Herman Perridan, found him in Opelousas, and shook his hand. We sat down and I listened to his story. When I asked him the question, "Herman, if you had to attribute your success to one thing, what would it be? Is it the food, is it the service? Is it the story you tell? Is it the fact that you are an African American in the segregated South serving white as well as black, sitting at the same table? What is it?" And without even blinking an eye, he said, "John, 'stickability,' stickability, that's the reason for my success." I looked at him. He said, "I am not even sure that's a word, but it's my word."

"Stickability, that's the reason for my success."

Herman Perridan

I asked him to tell me about that and he said, "John, today you look at young people coming through the restaurant, wanting to do what I do. The first thing they are not willing to give is time, they are not willing to sacrifice time and take these opportunities to learn, one day at a time. They want to learn everything today; they want to jump around from restaurant to restaurant because the new hot chef on the block is the guy who will teach them everything about success. They fail to realize that it's through sticking with your passion, and sticking with your education and sticking with opportunities that have [been] afforded you, one will ultimately learn everything they need to know to be successful. By devoting the time to your studies, the time to your apprenticeship, the time to your chef . . . that great knowledge will stick to your brain. Thereby you will never ever lose that day of education because you have devoted the time necessary to learn it. So John, if I had to say one thing, it would be stickability."

I asked him to tell me what I needed to do as a young restaurateur, how this stickability could apply to me. His answer was that first and foremost, you need to realize that when you go to work for an operator, you will have good and bad coming your way every day. You are going to be influenced by a lot of different situations, and just remember to stick to that place and take it all in. Then, be smart enough to discard what is not good and retain what is good, and stick to that place long enough, stick to that education long enough, to be able to value what is good and even what is not good. He went on to say, that is what young people refuse to do today. Buy that ticket of time and invest in that ticket of time. If you have enough time in a place, then even the bad things are a lesson, and you learn not to do those things again. You are going to learn to discard some things when you go down a path that doesn't work out for you.

He then said something to me that I will never forget: "Market your own uniqueness."

"Market your own uniqueness."

Herman Perridan

Every human being has a set of unique attributes. Find out what they are, whether it's the part of the country you are in, whether it's the family you were brought up in, or your social environment. But do remember this: Market that uniqueness and stick to that vision, and if you can do that then you will come out on the other side a winner, because nobody else can bring to the table what is unique about you. *That was the greatest life and work lesson I ever learned.*

That day in the very early 1980s, I adopted that philosophy of stickability. Whatever it is that you decide to do, give it enough time and stick to it. Give it a chance to be successful. If it's something that is unsuccessful, then learn from it.

I went home that night and immediately started to look at myself and assess what makes me different and unique compared to others. I took that lesson I learned that day and turned it into what is now Chef John Folse and Company. Then my goal was to share it with the world. It was at that point that I started to dream about opening restaurants in Russia, Japan, Italy. I didn't know how I was going to do it. I did not know where I was going to get the money. I just knew I could do it, and I did. It was that day, sitting with Herman Perriden, that I realized who I was going to be. That day changed my life and certainly was the beginning of Chef John Folse and Company, now 13 companies in all.

I have known Chef John Folse most of my professional career. I have heard that story at least three other times. But it wasn't until I heard the part about marketing your uniqueness, that I realized where John got his philosophy from. I am sure John could put his company in many other parts of the United States, areas that might be more profitable, where it might possibly be easier to obtain employees, easier to transport product via train and air, but John always stuck to his roots. He could place his restaurant and bed-and-breakfast properties in many different areas and certainly find places with better traffic, but John stayed to his roots for many reasons. That's who he is. He also has a mission to help as many people as possible along the way, including people in the small town where he grew up.

Dream—And Chase That Dream

Having a dream is a wonderful thing, but you can't just dream. You have to dream and then chase that dream with all your might. But how do you find your dream? How do you know when you find that one thing that makes you jump up out of bed in the morning and rush to it? How do we know when we find the thing we were put on this earth to do? I can't tell you what that is; only you will know. I can't dream it for you, I can't feel it for you, and I can't chase it for you. But you must be on the lookout for it. The lesson here is that you have to listen to what your heart is telling you. No dream is too small; no dream is too big. Nor do you need only one dream. Multiple dreams are all the more motivating.

One of my earliest dreams was to win a spot on the U.S. Culinary Olympic Team, which I achieved when I was twenty-three years old. Then my dream was to earn a Culinary Olympic gold medal, which I did the following year. Now, twenty years later, past member, coach, and manager of seven U.S. Culinary Olympic Teams and winner of numerous gold medals, I continue to dream and search and chase after that next thing that makes me jump out of bed in the morning.

If you are like me, you will find as you travel through life that you have talents you never knew you had. You have talents within yourself just begging to come out; you just have to listen to your heart, then work hard, never give up, and achieve. If you stumble or suffer setbacks along the way, it is only a message, a signal to say, "OK, now I know not to go this way." Say thank you, and take an alternate path to achieving the success you desire.

As Chef Folse shares with us, discover your uniqueness. How awesome is that statement? Everyone has something unique only to him or her. That one thing that makes you shine, that shine that makes other people say, "Hey, I don't know what you got, but please share it with me!" That shine that makes other people listen. Don't deprive yourself of this opportunity. Everyone's dream is different. It can be big or small. The important thing is to feel it. You will know it when you find it. It will excite you to the very core of your being. If it does not excite you in a way you have never experienced before, chances are this is not yet the dream you were made for. But don't discount any dreams. Your dreams are like a ladder—climb them all, because they are all tied together. One great dream leads to another. I would never have guessed twenty years ago, when competing for my first gold medal, that I would be sitting here writing books.

This is your time my friend. Start chasing!

Your Game Plan

What's your game plan? The purpose of this section is for you to start identifying your game plan for success. What are your goals, and how will you achieve them? This and all the chapters will include some things you can do to move your plans down the path toward success. By the time you finish this book, you will have your game plan.

- What are your dreams? Sort them out and write them down. Be looking for that one dream that just burns inside of you. You may have one, but you could also have many. Don't take your dreams for granted; take them seriously.

- What makes you unique? Think about how you are different from other people around you. How do you stand out from everyone else? Write your unique qualities down, and describe how they are going to help you define who you are, where you're going, and how you're going to get there.

- Given the dream or dreams you've identified, how long do you think it will take to achieve those dreams? While a number may change, set time goals for when you want to achieve your dreams. By doing this, you are setting your first goal—how long you think it will take to achieve this success.

Chapter Lessons

- Work like a champion, if you want to be a champion.
- To have the heart of a champion you must strive to be a champion.
- Think the way a champion thinks, if you truly want to achieve your goals and aspirations of being a champion.
- Be dedicated and committed like a champion, or nothing will happen.
- The only difference between the champions in this book and the average person is that the champions worked and trained relentlessly until they achieved the greatness they sought.
- Stickability! Stick to it.
- Market your uniqueness.

GEORGE FOREMAN

Boxer, Businessman, Minister

George Foreman

To interview Big George, the Champ, was an incredible and humbling experience. It is an experience to listen to a person so powerful yet so gentle. George Foreman established a record that most likely will never be broken. He is a two-time heavyweight champion of the world and an Olympic gold medalist. He became the oldest man ever to become heavyweight boxing champion of the world when, at age forty-five, he knocked out Michael Moorer to reclaim the title he held twenty years earlier. He is a successful businessman and an ordained Christian minister. Yet George Foreman never forgets where he came from and is always willing to help people.

George Foreman attributes much of his success to people who believed in him at a young age. He told me, "If you just keep working hard, you'll find that people will believe in you; then there is no limit to what you can obtain. That was the big lesson in life, people that believed in me and not just the boxing people. There was a lady in Oregon, her name was Mrs. Moon, who was a cook. She would drive all the way to California just to see how I was doing. She would always say, 'George, stop losing your temper, take care of your back and you will be OK.' It was people like Mrs. Moon that just believed in me and that's why I owe them so much. It's just meeting people in your life that believed in you. That's really what got me through."

> *"If you just keep working hard, you'll find that people will believe in you; then there is no limit to what you can obtain."*
> —George Foreman

He claims he started his boxing career on a dare. George was known for his bullying when he was younger. While watching the Cassius Clay (today, Muhammad Ali)–Floyd Patterson fight on television at the Job Corps, some of the other boys teased George and asked him, "Why don't you box, George? You're a bully. Why don't you become a boxer if you think you're so tough?" That challenge introduced the beginning of one of the greatest boxers of all times. As George told me, "Well, a lot of people believed in me, although I wanted mostly to take up boxing to further my bullying capacity. At first, after I tried it, I didn't really like it at all. I didn't like being in the ring."

The Champ had many challenges while growing up, mostly learning how to survive. He was known for his temper, which got in his way, keeping him from excelling. He soon realized he had to change if he was going to succeed at anything.

> *"If you know better, do better."*
>
> —George Foreman

George says, "I just always thought I had to be a tough guy. But then when I realized I couldn't beat the whole world up with my rage, I put down the losing of my temper and then, from that point on, success kept coming my way, one after another. I soon realized that I could take the same fists that got me into so much trouble and become a great athlete. I decided there was no need to fight anybody who was not a boxer. From that point on I just looked at the boxer, and the rage I had just disappeared; I just wasn't going to be a boxer beating up on people."

I admire George Foreman for many reasons, but what I am most fond of is his willingness to help young people. In 1983, George and his brother started the George Foreman Youth Center. He did everything he could to keep the center going, and that's what drove him back to boxing.

"I started a youth center to help kids, which used up all my life savings. Next thing you know, a kid gets himself out of trouble and then needs some money for college, books, and soon, every dime I had started to evaporate. I made up my mind I was not going to ask people to help me help kids. I decided I was going back into boxing to get the youth center going again. I hope I don't have to go into boxing again."

Imagine that. Going back into the ring to help other people. He did not do it for himself, he did it for the young people. Every dime he had ever earned went into helping young people. He put his body in harm's way to help others. You have to imagine for a second the training it takes to become heavyweight champion of the world, not to mention the training it takes a forty-five-year-old! The commitment of the Champ in my eyes is extraordinary.

"The easiest thing in the world is to earn a dollar. The hardest part is keeping that dollar, and I found that the best way is to keep earning. You have to constantly earn. I think a lot of young people and athletes who have their success so young forget that they have to continue to earn. You must earn, that's the lesson that's allowed me to survive."

George has a lot of interesting thoughts about working with today's children.

"Years ago when you saw kids slipping or falling down a well, it seemed easier to reach down and just pull them up. Now they are further away from you. It's more difficult to pick them up but it's obtainable. You just have to give them so much more of your time. One wrong move with kids, they can just fall farther than you can imagine and it's almost impossible to bring them back. I found out that with this [current] generation, you have to keep them closer to you, you have got to be more sincere than you have ever been before."

The Champ has ten children, and each of his five sons is named George: George Jr., George III, George IV, George V, and George VI. I asked him if he had a lack of creativity when naming the children.

"When you stand in the ring with the likes of Muhammad Ali, Joe Frazier, and Evander Holyfield and let them hit you on the head a couple hundred times . . . see how many names you can remember!

"My son, George Foreman III, we call him the Monk, he has had three professional matches so far. When he graduated from Rice University, he decided he wanted to be a boxer and I told all my kids, you can pursue whatever you want to pursue as long as you get a college education."

I asked the Champ what he thought his biggest accomplishment was. I just love his answer. It was not his first belt. It wasn't his second belt. It wasn't all of his victories or the Olympic gold medal.

"It's consistency in my work, whatever I do today, people have learned that I am going to be doing it tomorrow. What I say I am going to do, I am going to do."

Final words from George Foreman for everyone to live by:

"Dream big. Don't ever put brakes on your dreams. Dream big and anything you put your heart to you can obtain."

Chapter 2

Focusing on Your First Year at School

Embrace New Experiences

The first year of culinary school. What should you be thinking about? What should you be focusing on? What do you need to worry about, and what should you be taking advantage of? So many questions.

> "I would rather entertain and hope that people learned something than educate people and hope they were entertained."
>
> —Walt Disney

In today's world, education is hugely expensive. Please do not take this wonderful gift for granted, whether you are paying for school yourself, your family is paying for it, or you are on scholarship. To work hard for something is a good feeling. Achieving it is even more special. It is a great discipline to learn as a young person, so feel good about it and be proud of yourself.

> "Too many times with today's generation I find that students are looking for a degree and not an education. This is not the correct approach."
>
> —Dr. Rick Rigsby
> Author and nationally acclaimed speaker

Embrace New Experiences

Regardless of whether you are entering higher education straight from completing high school, you are a career changer going back to school, you are living away from home for the first time, or whatever your circumstances may be, it's important to make the most of your culinary educational experience. It's up to you to take responsibility for the decisions you make and the work you accomplish.

Your work ethic (sound familiar?) and time management skills will have a most significant impact on your success in culinary school and your first job in the kitchen.

CHOOSE YOUR FRIENDS WISELY

You will meet many people from all walks of life, both in school and on the job. This will be an exciting time in your life, as you will cultivate many new relationships and friendships. It's important to cultivate relationships that will help you achieve your goals. That's not to say you should not associate with anyone who cannot help you further your career. But it's important to stand strong against anyone or anything that may negatively influence your achievements.

> "I could have been a Rhodes Scholar, except for my grades."
>
> —Duffy Daugherty, Michigan State

Be particular with whom you hang out and with whom you study. They should have similar motivations to yours. One of the questions I get asked by students is, "How do you deal with other students in work groups not caring or not living up to their responsibilities to the group?" It is amazing to me that so many students are upset or disappointed in the effort, or lack of effort, of their peers. Group projects, both in the classroom and in the kitchen, are a common form of assignment and learning in education. If one or more members of the group do not hold up to their end of the workload, chances are, the whole group will suffer.

> "We can't solve problems by using the same kind of thinking we used when we created them."
>
> —Albert Einstein

So choose your friends wisely! Whether just starting school or your first kitchen position, you are laying the foundation for your future. If you rely on others to pull your weight, it will catch up to you very quickly. You want to control your own destiny.

> ## Control your own destiny.

It's as simple as that. You control your own destiny and make your own decisions. You want to be careful to make as many good decisions as possible. So *you* choose which road to take. Make the right choice. Ultimately, there is no one else to blame if you fail. Life is too short to be stupid. You can still have fun, just don't be stupid. You know the difference. Handle the challenges and responsibilities thrown at you like an adult, and make your family and loved ones proud of you.

> ## There is no one else to blame if you fail.

It is tempting at times to "take a walk on the wild side." But there are often consequences to doing so. Instead, choose friends with whom you have something in common and who are as serious about their education as you are. These are the people who will make you a better student; together, all of you as a team can be even stronger. This can be a powerful tool that will help you grow. Not only will you get the advantages of education and research from other people in your group, but you will also form bonds and friendships that will most likely stay with you throughout your career and the rest of your life.

DEVELOP A LEADERSHIP TEAM

Here is a great idea for you to enhance your personal education and strengthen your net worth as a culinarian. During the beginning months of your education, take a look around at the friends that you are meeting. Take a close look at the work ethic and overall professionalism of some of the students you most admire. Carefully select a few friends who you believe are very successful in school, ones you can imagine being very successful when they graduate. Find these students who are taking their education seriously and start your own "Leadership Team" study group. Invite three or four of these students to a quick meeting and carefully introduce this idea to them.

By starting this team, you now can pool your hard work and resources together as one. You all share the same passion for success and take your time at school seriously. Why not join your individual and collective strengths together? Remember, none of you is as smart as all of you! You can do your homework together, share your research with each other, and cover more ground as a group. Understand that the reason for this group is to become elite, not to ditch homework, or to do less work, or to finish quicker. The true reason is to make your education more powerful, to receive four times the information because you have now pooled your resources. In fact, you may find that you, as a group, are working harder and longer than other individuals. Imagine how the net worth of your education will grow.

RESEARCH YOUR TOP FOUR STAR CHEFS

A big part of defining your road to success is trying to find out what it is you want to do. What kind of chef do you want to be? What kind of property do you want to work in? How do you get there? Some of you may want to work in a fine dining restaurant, catering, pastry, hotels, clubs, and so on. The list can be endless. As you start to feel your way through school, try to identify chefs you most admire—chefs you think you want to be like. Start looking in magazines and cookbooks of chefs you most connect with.

As a soul-searching exercise, challenge your Leadership Team to identify four chefs they think they most want to emulate, or to follow in the footsteps of their careers. Your Leadership Team will now research what has made these chefs successful, what road they took toward their success. What were their failures, what were their challenges, what were their secrets, who were their mentors? Research their complete background. Try to interview them by phone. Share with the chefs that it is for a school project, and they will help. After each of you has completed this information, you should have sixteen incredible resources about great chefs—all the ins and outs of what has made these chefs so special. You now are much more educated about their talent, which will possibly help you further define what kind of chef you want to be.

Imagine the possibilities and strengths of this group. You should make this group exclusive and "Yours." Don't allow distractions. Have fun with it, come up with a name for your group. You can use this research technique with any educational advancement you can think of. Use this exercise for researching different kinds of jobs for externships, opportunities after graduation, styles or regions of cooking. Share some of this research with some instructors you most bond with. The possibilities are endless.

And, oh yeah, this group will work together on homework too. I love this idea. Can't you just taste the success?

ADVICE FROM CULINARY EDUCATORS

Q: *What advice do you offer for the student on the first day of school?*

A: To reach an objective, it must be clearly identified so subsequent actions lead toward its achievement. You must take the time to clearly identify your short-term school goals, and long-term career goals. Actually listing the goals before starting classes will help you focus on them. Each decision and action will take you closer toward realizing your goals. Then, although it rests with you to advance your own career, immediately surround yourself with quality people who have your best interests in mind. Whether they are mentors, teachers, or peers, these people will become your support group as you proceed through school and into the industry.

Robert Garlough, MS, AAC
Founding Director of the Grand Rapids Community College
Secchia Institute for Culinary Education

A:

- Be on time
- Be prepared to work
- Make sure your uniform is clean and pressed
- Take notes
- Always ask questions
- Crawl before you walk and walk before you run

Chef Paul Sorgule, CEC, AAC
Provost, New England Culinary Institute

A: Go to class. Most students don't realize the value of lost time. Participate. School is no different than most things in life—you get out of it what you put into it. Envision Success: Know where you are going—work hard to get there and remain true to your core values. Don't let anyone or anything derail your personal plan. Have fun. If you love what you do you will never work another day in your life.

Chef Kirk T. Bachmann, M.Ed., CEC, CCP
Vice President of Academics,
Le Cordon Bleu Schools of North America

The greatest challenge for culinary students today is to stay focused on developing their cooking and knife skills.

Really developing these skills requires repetition and lots of sincere, hard work.

Mainstream celebrities, foodies, and nonprofessionals constantly offer very confusing images of what a chef is. Students will often adopt these random ideas and other weak standards, such as poor sanitation. Most chefs and teachers have to deal with "undoing" or working around the bad habits and poor skills students have developed, before a real professional cooking experience can begin.

For students to overcome this, they should make a decision early on. Do they want to be the star pitcher of the little league, or a key player in the major leagues . . . then, take the steps to gain employment in a major-league-level establishment that has a world-class reputation for food. Existing in that environment will be a lot more comfortable, especially if good cooking is what you want to do for your livelihood. Working in good establishments means that you will be working with other experts who have specialized service and creative talents, management, and leadership methods you can learn from.

Daniel Hugelier CMC
Schoolcraft Community College

When I left for school, my dad said something to me that has stuck with me to this day:

"Never be afraid of what you know, and don't be afraid of what you don't know."

This quote may not mean much to you yet, but let me explain why it has stayed with me for so long. I grew up in a country inn, in Waterford, Vermont. When you own a business, it seems there are no days off. I took two years of culinary arts in high school, and after I graduated I worked at the Balsams Grand Resort for two years. During this time, I worked every department, receiving an incredible wealth of experience. By the time I left for culinary school, I had a decent "rookie" foundation. These opportunities allowed me to appreciate and understand the things the instructors were teaching more than someone with less or no experience.

Even with this experience, I was still scared out of my mind walking into college. I was overwhelmed by the school and intimidated by all the upperclassman and all their experience. My point is, even with all the experience

I had entering the school, which was probably more than 90 percent of my class had, I was still scared. For me, reaching back and remembering what my father told me gave me confidence walking down the hallways and going to class. Never be afraid of what you know. I relied on what little experience I had to get me through each day.

> "Before anything else, preparation is the key to success."
> —Alexander Graham Bell

THIS IS YOUR TIME TO BE A STUDENT

You may see some attitudes in students spreading their wings and thinking they already know everything they need to know of the culinary world. Don't let them intimidate you. Be yourself and understand that this is your time to be a student and learn from everyone. This is your time to learn as much as you possibly can. You don't have to have all the answers now, so take advantage of "what you don't know." Don't be afraid of what you don't know. Don't be afraid to challenge your instructors or ask them questions. Get your money's worth while you are in school. Stand tall and ask questions. Chances are, all the questions you ask many other students are thinking but are too afraid to ask, or are too afraid to show what they don't know.

> Understand, this is your time to be a student. Take advantage of what you don't know.

To this day I am not afraid of what I don't know. I rely on my staff to help me with what I don't know. I ask my team of experts their opinions, the ones who are on the firing line working hard. I believe this is what makes our team so strong; I rely on the talents of my staff. But I also will tell you another secret: What inspires me every day is what I don't know! This is what drives me to want to become better as a chef and a culinarian.

> What inspires me every day is what I don't know.

Volunteer, Get Involved

Step up and volunteer, get involved. You are in school to set the pace for the rest of your life, and you need to understand that. You're not in school to party. Yes, have fun, but understand your responsibilities as an adult, and the first one is to learn. Too many times I have seen new culinarians sit on the sidelines and miss out. Too many times I have seen young chefs punch in for their shift, punch out when it is time to go home, and have no clue as to what was actually going on that day. Not only do they have no clue, they don't care to have a clue. Don't punch in and punch out and wonder why you're never getting ahead.

> "No one can make you feel inferior without your consent."
>
> —Eleanor Roosevelt

While at school, as a student, you need to dive into any experiences available to you. Seek out and find out what is going on around you. Volunteer for special events, special dinners, or occasions when visiting chefs come in to speak. Get involved with special groups or competitions. Get involved with the student body and different committees and clubs. Don't graduate only to look back and regret that you didn't take full advantage of the opportunities you were given. The more experiences you are a part of, the more valuable you are as a chef or manager. The more experiences, the more accomplished you become. Don't punch in and punch out of school, never getting involved, and then wonder why you don't know what is going on around you. Wonder why those who do get involved are more recognized by their peers.

When I was in school, I was interested in competing and wanted to learn as much as I could about the U. S. Culinary Olympic Team. When I was in high school, I entered a few local competitions, so I had the bug. Then, when I went to culinary school and saw some of the very chefs I had seen in Olympic cookbooks and in videos, I was star struck. I would chase these chefs down the hallway. I would ask them millions of questions. I would beg them to let me volunteer for anything. I wanted to be on a Culinary Olympic Team so bad I could taste it. Do you see what I am saying? That's the "chewing off the end of the table" mentality. I would not let my energy and enthusiasm be denied . . . and it wasn't.

OPPORTUNITY THAT CHANGED MY LIFE

The school I attended decided to enter a professional team in the New York Restaurant Show, food competition. They assembled a team of instructors and started planning and preparing for a Grand Buffet category, which is a very large display of several categories. The school then asked for volunteers for a student apprentice team to assist all the chefs. This was it! My chance to get involved with some of my heroes, some of the chefs I most respected. This was my chance to finally work with these culinary geniuses.

This commitment was a lot of work, but it was my dream to be on a culinary team. The apprentices got all the clean-up jobs, peeling jobs, and sometimes, if they were talented enough, they got the opportunity to tourné two hundred root vegetables so the chef could pick out the eight most perfect ones and throw the rest in a stock pot. I made it on this student team and worked all hours of the night with two of the most talented master chefs in our Culinary Olympic history, Chefs Tim Ryan and Mark Erickson. Just having the opportunity to work with these two talents and see firsthand the secrets of Culinary Olympic competition was truly the stepping stone to my competition life. Working, volunteering, experiencing, and learning with these chefs helped pave *my* road to success. I learned more in those two weeks about culinary competition than I had learned in the past three years. This experience alone was the beginning of my Culinary Olympic career. Now twenty-four years later, I am a proud member of eight world Culinary Olympic teams.

> "Working, volunteering, experiencing, and learning with these great chefs helped pave my road to success."

I often wonder what my career would be like today if I had decided to go partying with my friends instead of volunteering for the apprentice team. Imagine if I had decided that personal time was more valuable to me than working long hours peeling vegetables for some competition. *"What if . . . ?"* I have no doubt whatsoever it would be completely different than it is now. Competing on a national and international level, representing the United States in a world arena has changed my life. I truly believe that being on Culinary Olympic teams has opened many doors and opportunities for me that I am forever grateful for.

What opportunities are out there for you? What opportunities are you missing? "What if" you volunteer for something that will change your life or help you pave your road to success? Can you imagine how powerful the tool of volunteering is? To volunteer for anything while you are in school will be an education and an experience for you. Even if you hate a particular experience, you will learn from it.

> Imagine how powerful the tool of volunteering is.

The Power of Networking

The power of networking is immeasurable. We will talk about this at great length later in the book, but I want to touch on it now. Volunteering while you're in school will allow you to meet all kinds of people you would not have met otherwise. Volunteering will allow other professionals to view your passion and energy. Volunteering gives you an opportunity to network with individuals in the industry who, oftentimes, will help you with your future. Every opportunity to bond with a chef or mentor outside of school hours you must take. Gaining as many contacts as possible at any point in your career will aid you for many years to come.

> The power of networking is immeasurable.

So volunteer! Only great things happen when you volunteer! Give yourself an opportunity to *win*. Give yourself an opportunity to *win* an edge toward your own growth and road map to success. Do it now! Do it while you are in school or in your first job. Take advantage of all the resources available to you, including volunteering.

> Give yourself an opportunity to win.

Your Game Plan

What's your game plan? Add the following items to the game plan you are creating for yourself.

- Who are the students or kitchen workers you think you will excel with and learn from? Identify a group of people you think you can be great friends with and trust. Look for a group that will be very astute, take care of each other, and have fun together as well. Your support group is very important to your success.

- Read the bulletin boards and look for opportunities to volunteer. Talk to your instructors to find ways to get involved. Don't overload yourself at the beginning, but start your networking and get involved! Find one thing that you can do in the next month. The more you volunteer, the more you network; the more you network, the more experience you get; the more experience you get, the more you're worth. The more you network, the more you will get the fantastic opportunities you could only dream about before.

Chapter Lessons

- Choose your friends wisely. Surround yourself with great people.
- Control your own destiny.
- There is nobody else to blame if you fail.
- Be aware of your surroundings at all times.
- Don't be afraid to challenge or ask questions.
- Volunteer and get involved as much as possible.
- Don't look back only to regret that you should have worked harder or taken advantage of more opportunities.
- Network with other chefs and students as often as possible.

PAUL PRUDHOMME

Louisiana Restaurateur and Creator of Magic Seasoning Blends®

The Legend

Paul Prudhomme
Photo © Michael Palumbo

The man and legend Chef Paul Prudhomme has given America and the world a style of food that is here to stay. Blackening is Chef Paul's claim to fame. He became the face of New Orleans in the early 1980s, and he has hung on ever since. He was a fixture on *Good Morning America* and *The Today Show* for many years, to which he attributes much of his success. To be honest, he is being very humble; we all need a little luck from time to time, but Chef Paul's success came from a great deal of hard work and a tremendous amount of perseverance.

Here is a man who is incredibly successful with his landmark K-Paul's Restaurant and his Magic Seasoning Blends®. He is the man who single-handedly put Cajun Creole cuisine on the map. The plastic bags of seasonal blends his patrons insisted on buying at the restaurant are now distributed in thirty-eight countries. We all know the successful Chef Paul. Let me share with you his story of what led to his success.

I asked him how he first got interested in cooking.

"I was the thirteenth child in a family of farmers that didn't have gas or electricity and cooked on a wood-burning stove. There were three girls and ten boys and as soon as the three girls were married and moved on, my father said, 'You have to help me with the chores.' The whole family had to sit down at the same time and eat together and if you didn't show up on time you didn't eat! That was the rule and that was a wonderful thing to see everybody sitting together and eating dinner. It was from this experience I realized how powerful food was and how good-tasting food can just turn the whole thing around, everyone just stopped arguing and just enjoyed the food."

I am wondering how many culinarians would have been passionate about cooking if they had grown up without electricity or gas, no dishwashers, and fifteen mouths to feed. If you did not show up for dinner, you lost because the rest of the hardworking family ate, and they ate well. In fact, I have heard stories from those with large families, that even if you were present at the table but you were not paying attention, you could lose out on your portion. Chef Paul discovered at a very early age the power of food and how it brings people together.

Chasing his Dream

Chef Paul went on to tell me, "I always wanted to have my own restaurant and I did the first year, right out of high school. The family helped me do it, [but] it was not a success. The next three restaurants also failed. Every time I failed I didn't think of it as a bad thing, I looked at it as a lesson, and it was these lessons and the enormous amount of information which led to the success of K-Paul's. [It] is a wonderful restaurant, everything is fresh; in fact we don't even have ice-cream because we don't have any freezers. The best thing you can do for another human being is to provide them with a fantastic meal. It's always been my mission in life to put great food in people's bodies."

> "Every time I failed I didn't think of it as a bad thing, I looked at it as a lesson, and it was these lessons and the enormous amount of information which led to the success of K-Paul's."
>
> —Chef Paul Prudhomme

"I married my first wife a few months before my first restaurant opened and one day I was sitting on a rocking chair on my father's porch and I was thinking about all the things that had gone wrong. I realized my wife didn't want to be in the restaurant business. I realized everything that I liked wasn't necessarily what everybody else liked and if you didn't take care of the food you would lose it. As the third restaurant came and went away I ended up moving to Colorado and opened up three restaurants, which all became successful. I decided to come home when my mom found out she had cancer. I started working in restaurants to get the money to build my own. I worked on oil rigs, offshore because it was really good money. Then, my late wife Kay, and I decided to open up our own restaurant, which still exists today, K-Paul's, and is thirty years old now."

Think about what Chef Paul said here. He had three restaurants, all of which failed. Think about how much effort goes into the opening of one restaurant, let alone three. Three in a row failed. What do you think you would have done? Imagine if Chef Paul had quit after any of the first three. Our culinary world would be different, wouldn't it? There would be no

Magic Seasoning Blends®, and there probably wouldn't be any blackening techniques. The lessons from the champions continue to shine through! Keep working, keep working, work a little harder, and things will work out for you. Chef Paul never gave up.

Chef Paul's Lessons

Chef Paul talked a lot about the lessons he learned. "The most important lesson that I learned was to stay true to yourself and don't lie to yourself, don't beat up on other people because you made a mistake or if they made a mistake. I love people and I love to get the best out of them for themselves and it has paid me off amazingly. It didn't happen overnight to have the philosophy that I have; I gained [it] over a fifty-year time period."

> *"Be true to yourself and if you can't do it now, then keep working at it until you can do it."*
>
> —Chef Paul Prudhomme

"We all learn from each other and it's a continuous learning curve. To give you an example how fanatic I am about food, I have someone who is the president of my seasoning company as well as the restaurant. This is so I can be involved with the food and the research and development. It is my job to cook and taste every day. I continually try to work on new flavors, as that's what the company was built on and that's my job."

I asked Chef Paul about the most rewarding time in his life.

"I think it's yet to come. Of all the things that happened to me, I can't pick one out. Each one was a step in my life and not all of them were good; it was part of the learning curve.

"I lost four restaurants in a row but it was never a bad thing for me. It was always, man, look what I learned. Being the last of thirteen children was an experience, I had seven brothers that were in WWII.

"Be true to yourself and if you can't do it now, then keep working at it until you can do it."

There can be no truer words.

Chapter 3

Work Ethic and Habits

No Orange Hands!

Your work ethic will dictate your success! End of story. Well, there's actually more to it than this basic statement, but it is a good credo to have in mind as you shape yourself into the kind of culinarian you want to be. And it's a philosophy that should stay with you throughout your culinary education and work experience. Your work ethic will be a large part of what defines you to those you work with throughout your career.

The purpose of this chapter is to share with you how to be successful in school and the early part of your work experience. The first step is to begin working on one of the most important values you can apply to your professional life: your work ethic. Your work ethic will dictate your success by helping you gain the respect of your fellow culinarians, earn top grades, win the job of your choice, win the promotion of your dreams, climb the professional ladder faster, and gain trust from your boss.

> "Opportunity is missed by most people because it is dressed in overalls and looks like work."
>
> —Thomas Edison

This chapter appears at the beginning of this book because you need to start NOW! You need to start working on establishing an uncompromising level of work ethic now. You need to start these practices while you are in school and getting your beginning work experiences, because all of this will help you be successful.

> You need to start working on establishing an uncompromising level of work ethic now.

Work Ethic and Habits

I can't make it any more black and white than that. Your work ethic and your work habits will dictate your success. Period. The sooner you understand this, the quicker you will be on the path to success. So if you know you have a terrible work ethic, you need to determine whether you are willing to change it, and what you are willing to do to change it. The one promise I can make is that if you don't develop a successful work ethic, you will not succeed in this or any other profession. You need to be willing to "chew off the end of the table to be successful." I would hire a student who has an incredible work ethic with no experience before I would hire a hotshot chef with years of experience but a lousy work ethic. To me that's a no brainer.

> Your work ethic and your work habits will dictate your success. Period.

Again, there's a reason this is one of the first chapters in the book. Defining what your work ethic and work habits will be is the first step on the path to success. No matter how smart you are, how computer savvy you've become, how high your grades are, or the number of recipes you've collected, if you're not willing to put in the effort, if you're not willing to learn and absorb everything that comes your way—whether in the classroom or in the kitchen—success will be fleeting. I may sound like a broken record, but it is really that simple.

WASTED TALENT

I have known a lot of chefs, many students, and externs who had great talent, knew they had great talent, and wasted it all, or at the very least hampered their professional advancement, because they had a terrible work ethic. It's also important to maintain an appropriate work ethic. I have seen managers who once had a great work ethic, but once they become a boss, it was as if they shut it off. It was as if they said to themselves, "Hey I made it, now I am going to coast."

I specifically remember one instance when we had a recent intern from a local hospitality school working for the club. This student was incredibly focused and driven. He had a clear goal of wanting to learn as much about the hospitality field as possible. This intern started out as a waiter in banquets and then worked his way up to bartender. After graduation he started as manager of our pool restaurant, which is a very busy part of our operation. I love this job as a stepping-stone for all new managers or recent graduates, whether they are culinary or front-of-the-house management. For me, pool chef is the first rung in the ladder of gaining a position in my kitchen. If you are next in line for a sous chef position, the first big job you get is pool chef.

So the intern, now graduated and a full-time employee, did a fantastic job by the pool. The pool that year ran better than it ever had, because he cared. He cared about his job, cared about all of his employees, and genuinely cared about the level of service. He worked hard, too. He was always the first one in and the last one to leave. As a young person, one of the biggest secrets you can learn is to earn the respect of your staff and supervisors. Another secret here is to understand that it does not make a difference if you are serving a peanut butter and jelly sandwich or a twelve-course gourmet dinner, both are just as important to the property and the guest. The sooner all chefs and cooks understand that, the sooner they will be successful. It is the attention to the smallest of details that truly makes a special person. No job is too small or less important than the other.

After the summer season, the intern was on his way to success. He worked long hours and was promoted to beverage manager. Now, this is a big job with lots of responsibilities. He worked hard for another three or four months but soon began to slip. His work ethic became unrecognizable from the one we once knew. Once he received the job he wanted, the pay, the office, and the respect, he changed the way he worked. His negative attitude toward service and the way he treated his staff were not appropriate.

We never found out why his attitude changed, but it ended up costing him his job. Once you get to your goal, once you reach the position you so desired, you don't stop! Now that you're there, make a difference! Don't settle for the status quo, make a difference, make it better, improve on everything you touch.

Don't change jobs, change the way you do your job. Don't change your work habits and work ethic once you finally achieve one of your goals. Always remember what got you the job to begin with.

There's no resting on your laurels. Your work ethic needs to continue and evolve as you make your way through your career. I have seen brilliant culinary school graduates, with lots of talent, work in industry for eight months and think they "have it." But once they move on to take their first executive chef job, more often than not they fail. And 99.9 percent of the time, this failure can be attributed to terrible work habits, no work ethic, and no experience. I call this talented waste.

- Show up early for work, READY and focused for the day.
- Want to know WHY, want to know more than the job at hand, want to know what's going on around you.
- Never find yourself lazy or too comfortable; if you're comfortable, you're not looking hard enough to improve.
- If promoted, don't be content with maintaining; your goal should be to improve the current environment.

Good Employee

It frustrates me to no end that in today's environment, what many consider to be a good employee is simply one who *shows up on time* and does what he or she is asked to do. Isn't that sad? To think that today's standard of what makes a good employee has sunk so low is disheartening. I recognize that often just getting someone to take a job seriously enough to arrive on time can be a task. But it's what you try to inspire in those who work for and with you that can be one of your greatest assets and what can set you apart from everyone else.

When I was growing up, if you were fifteen minutes early, you were already thirty minutes late. Today is much different. Will the employee who thinks it's OK to be late now and again get the first opportunity to be promoted? Probably not. I can't tell you how many times I have seen this. During the performance review they want to know why they can't get more money or why they are constantly being passed over for a promotion.

> If you are fifteen minutes early, you are already thirty minutes late.

"I WANT MORE MONEY"

So many times I conduct a performance review with an employee who has been late from time to time. These are what I consider "punch in, punch out" employees, meaning they are there simply to get a paycheck. They do not have any real interest in creating wonderful food; their only goal is to get the food on the table.

During reviews, they would ask, "Chef, why can't I get more money?" In many cases, I would be giving them a standard pay raise, but they felt it was not enough. I would ask them how many times they had been late over the past year, then show them their documented record of warnings and late arrivals. Then I ask what they have done this past year that has benefited their career. What have they done to grow? What have they done to increase their self-worth as a professional? What have they done differently this year above and beyond what they did last year, or are they simply doing the same job? If their progress today is the same as a year ago, why should I pay them more? If they have not worked hard to push themselves to be better, why should I pay more?

> What have you done to increase your self-worth as a professional?

What does it take to be a great employee? If all it takes is to simply show up on time, it can't be that difficult to do a little more. So what can you do? How can you work on your work ethic and work habits? Start at this very moment to identify what you want your work ethic and work habits to be. And once you've determined what your practice will be, start putting it to work right now. Creating or identifying your goal is not enough. An ethic or habit is something you do over and over and over again. That is why it becomes a habit. We have good habits and bad habits. What we want to identify are fantastic work practices and make them habits.

> Identify fantastic work practices and make them habits.

Ethic

> "1. The discipline of dealing with what is good and bad and with moral duty and obligations. 2. A set of moral principles or values. 3. The practice of conforming to accepted professional standards of conduct."
>
> —Merriam-Webster Dictionary

Professional standards and personal standards of how we conduct ourselves on a daily basis are vitally important to your success. So you need to practice to be great, practice to work clean, practice a great work ethic, and practice great habits. You can't just flip on a switch and be great. You have to develop these standards and habits over time and continue working at and improving them. What follows are some tools, some concepts that will make you successful if you practice them! These practices are exciting because they make sense and they are practical.

LESSON #1: KNOW THE JOB

> Get to know the job better than the person teaching you.

Whether you are at home with your parents, at school with your instructors, or working several stations in your workplace, if you have this attitude you will be successful. Whether in a school kitchen or workplace, you will be trained on dozens of different stations, tasks, and jobs. If you attack every job with the attitude that you will come to know the job better than the person training you, do you think you will excel at that position? If your goal is to learn a department as well as the department head, will you be considered a "punch in, punch out" employee? I don't think so. If your goal is to be in charge when your boss is out, chances are you will care a whole lot about your work. As a result, your boss will be impressed with your attitude and your maturity of wanting more responsibility.

> "Students need to learn how to think critically, how to argue opposing ideas. It is important for them to learn how to think. You can always cook."
>
> —Charlie Trotter

To accomplish this you have to ask yourself questions: What is my boss doing now? What is he reading? Why does the chef want things done a certain way? How does she figure out the percentages of food to order? How, how, how, why, why, why!

> "I remember when I was in college, I used to watch Julia Child's cooking show during dinner and joke with my roommates about becoming a TV chef."
>
> —Martin Yan

This is where your work ethic and habits come in. If you are not disciplined with your work ethic and work habits, if you do not demonstrate your capabilities and talent, you will not receive the acknowledgment and recognition you are seeking.

Early in my executive chef career, we had a student intern who was working with our buffet chef. The two of them were in charge of all the hot food for lunch buffets every day that would feed anywhere from two hundred to five hundred people. This student was on fire. He wanted to know everything he possibly could about all the food they were using. He was interested in the farms the ingredients came from. He even went to visit the local farmers on his own time. When the buffet chef was off, he would run the station. This student worked hard and became involved with the menus. On his days off he would learn how to carve ice with other chefs. In the middle of the summer, the buffet chef fell ill and had to take a long-term, extended absence, and would not return for the rest of the season. This student intern, who was due to graduate after his internship was over, was the one left holding the keys. This was his chance to shine, work hard, develop menus, step up, and run the station. Because he was so driven to know the station, and genuinely interested in all aspects of the job, he was able to take over a sous chef job as a student.

Sometimes being in the right place at the right time makes a big difference, but unless you're focused and care, care about your own education, you will never be in the right place to begin with.

Don't Be Lazy

You make the choice. Make the decision to work hard. Motivate yourself. You will end up waiting a long time if you wait for others to motivate you. Don't complain about your surroundings. You can choose to be lazy, or you can choose to take action. Discipline yourself to do something about what you don't like. If you don't, all you're doing is gaining a reputation as a complainer.

> Motivate yourself; don't wait for others to motivate you.

That attribute of *not* being lazy is so admirable. I can find *lazy* every day. The world is full of lazy. The world is full of mediocre. I have to look past many people to find energy, discipline, and fantastic follow-through in a person. And once I do, I take notice of and pleasure in working with and alongside that chef.

> That attribute of not being lazy is so admirable. The world is full of lazy. The world is full of mediocre.

LESSON #2: FOLLOW THROUGH

> Possess uncompromising levels of follow-through.

Weak follow-through is one of my pet peeves. Follow-through is everything! It means not only that you're not lazy, but that you are reliable and dependable.

The most frustrating part of my job is having to go behind employees to be sure they have completed their task 100 percent. If I have to constantly check up on the same employees time after time, they soon fall low on the ladder. Conversely, if I give instruction to an employee and this person not only completes the task, but completes it above and beyond my expectations . . . WOW! Which employee do you think I consider to be a superstar?

WHAT GOES AROUND COMES AROUND

This is a motto I have lived by for many years. Good things happen to good people. If you work hard with a can-do attitude, constantly pushing to improve, you will be recognized and rewarded. If you wake up every morning and say to yourself, "I am going to work hard and do the best I can today," you will. If you constantly have a positive outlook on life, every day, positive things will come back to you. If you work hard every day to help other people, if you don't leave work until you have helped somebody else do his or her job, many people will help you in return. You will receive what you give, only in larger quantities. So give big, help big, be positive in a large way, and you will be rewarded. What goes around comes around.

When I first started as an executive chef at a new property, I was all fired up to make change and start building my new team. There were a million things I wanted to accomplish, many ideas and concepts to put into place that would, in my mind, make for a better operation. When your to-do list is pages long, you need help to accomplish it all. You have to trust your staff and empower them to succeed, or you will fail yourself. I was very lucky that my sous chef at the time was incredibly focused and disciplined. I would sometimes give him a long list of things to accomplish for the week, and he always completed it. Not only did he complete the list, but he always finished each job better than my expectations.

This was one of my first epiphanies in my professional chef career. You have to learn to trust your people because you can't do it all yourself. The more he achieved, the more I gave him. My sous chef taught me a lot. I trusted him with everything and because his work ethic was second to none, I would bend over backwards for him. Whatever he needed or wanted, I helped him get it. I eventually had to say good-bye to him. He was too good to be a sous chef all his life. I made sure that he got the best job he possibly could get. I wanted to be sure to help him in any way I could. Remember, what goes around comes around!

I can't tell you what a great feeling it is when you ask someone to do something and it is completed 100 percent. To know and trust without a doubt that the follow-through of your employee is so dedicated and true, you never have to go back and check to see if it was done. This person would never, ever take a shortcut or take the easy road and sacrifice quality, which many times is a temptation for less-motivated employees. Ladies and gentlemen, in my mind, this is one of the most admirable attributes one can ever have, 100 percent follow-through and trust. This is the characteristic of a great person.

LESSON #3: EXCEED EXPECTATIONS

> Complete each task above and beyond all expectations.

One day the chef asks Joey to peel a fifty-pound bag of carrots. Joey whines that he just peeled a bag yesterday. He complains that it took him almost an hour and a half the day before, and he is supposed to punch out in an hour.

"Why do I always have to peel the carrots?" Joey asks. "I always get stuck with the dumb jobs."

What kind of attitude does Joey have? Do you think this attitude will get Joey far in the hospitality field? I don't think so.

Yes, there are many jobs in the kitchen that are less fun than others. So how can Joey look at this job differently? How can Joey complete a simple task today and improve his skills and knowledge with the bag of carrots? How about trying to beat his peeling time from yesterday? He can set up his station better so it is more systematic. Joey's goal should be to train someone else at this station if needed. His goal should be to know the station better than the person teaching him.

> "I wanted to learn everything I could about what it takes to be a great chef. It was a turning point for me."
>
> —Thomas Keller

He can find out from the chef what the carrots are for. If they are for a carrot timbale, he can get the formula to add to the resources he is building while on this station. What function are the carrot timbales for? Maybe Joey can make a case to the chef to let him prepare the timbales tomorrow because he has never made them before. Joey can familiarize himself with the rest of the menu. On and on we can go. All from a bag of carrots. If your attitude is just to peel carrots, all you'll end up with is orange hands.

> If your attitude is just to peel carrots, all you will end up with is orange hands.

The purpose of this exercise is for you to ask questions. You have to ask questions to get answers. If your instructor or boss asks something of you, the first question should be how you can complete this task above and beyond all expectations. If you do this, you're now on the road to success.

So What Is Your Work Ethic?

I expect all my sous chefs to think like executive chefs. I give them the freedom to make their own decisions. You have to practice to be something before you can become it. You can't just turn on the switch one day and decide to be responsible. You have to be responsible from the get-go. All of this falls under your work ethic and work habits.

> I expect all my chefs to think like executive chefs.

In the end, it turns out it is very simple to separate yourself from the pack. It is very easy to separate yourself from just simply being good, to being great.

> Your work ethic should be so incredible, so focused, so intense that you will never be passed over for a position or promotion. You will never be denied.

Your work ethic will dictate your success, period!
End of story.
Don't end up with orange hands.

Your Game Plan

What's your game plan? Add the following items to the game plan you are creating for yourself.

- Identify three points that describe your work ethic. What is it currently? What do you want it to be? Be honest with yourself. Recognize when you are being lazy or are feeling unmotivated, and do something about it.
- Show up early for work and for school. The more you do this, the more it will become habit. If you are early for class and your instructor is there, take advantage of that time to visit with him or her.
- Finish everything you start. Classroom projects, homework, workplace assignments, etc. When presented with a task, turn it into an opportunity and finish it in a way you believe is beyond what was expected of you. Identify a task you have to accomplish this week and formulate your plan for completing it above and beyond expectations.

Chapter Lessons

So here's what you need to do to begin establishing your work ethic and work habits:

- Develop an uncompromising work ethic that becomes habit.
- Show up early to work or class, ready to go!
- Strive to know the job better than the person teaching you.
- Don't be lazy.
- Motivate yourself; don't wait for others to motivate you.
- Follow through.
- Complete each task above and beyond all expectations.
- Whatever level of experience you have, ALWAYS try to think like an executive chef.
- Your work ethic will dictate your success.

BELA KAROLYI

United States Women's Gymnastic Olympic Team Coach

Going for Gold

Bela Karolyi, the most successful and recognized Olympic gymnastics coach in the world today, has a special story of survival and perseverance. As you read, imagine yourself in his shoes. What would you have done to survive?

Bela Karolyi

My Dream

Bela told me, "Sports was an obsession of mine ever since I was in middle school. I grew up in far away Romania where opportunities at that time were few. My father was opposed to my interest in sport activities. He was a civil engineer and had a different mindset, so as a young person I got it in my heart, in my head, in my dreams, hoping to become a successful sports person. Already, at a very young age, I somehow knew I wanted to be a coach. As I was going through my challenges, I realized how much I needed someone strong, someone to support me, encouraging hands to coach me, which I missed out on. I decided that when I graduated from a university I wanted to be a coach in a way that I knew a coach should be.

"After graduating from high school, I tried to make a living in sports, doing whatever I could to survive. I tried boxing, soccer, water polo, and track and field. Back then, the college arena really wasn't a way to make a living. So when I had the opportunity, I made an attempt to work in the University of Physical Education of Romania, which I finally managed to do. So this is where I got involved with the sport of gymnastics, which was mandatory. Then I realized, here is a sport that is totally different than anything I had ever studied before. Here is sport which gives you an unbelievable insight to who you really are. It's not just about the physical aspect but also the moral aspect, the desire, the determination and all those very important factors in our lives. It's a sport that has amazing character building, which I thought was important as a young person.

"I met my wife at the university; [she] was a high performer in the sport of gymnastics. I had never been a high performer but she was one of the top competitors, the national champion of her time. I was working very hard to make my presence felt on the university team, which I was able to do. Gymnastics became a sport I was very focused on."

Everyone has a different relationship with their parents. Some relationships are very close, some are challenging. Some people lack parental guidance, some are from split families, and some are missing a parent altogether. No one person has the exact same situation as another. Bela's challenge was that his father did not want him to go into sports as a profession. This can be very stressful for a young person who has a particular dream. I can't tell you what is right or wrong. I can't tell you what decision to make. All I can say is to follow your dream. Follow what is in your heart and listen to what it is telling you. As they say: If you do what you love, you'll never work a day in your life. In this case, Bela went after his dream and listened to what his heart told him, but it came with great pain and hard work. I asked him what he felt his biggest challenge in life was.

"Remember, never to forget, what is your dream, what is your life, what is your beloved profession."

—Bela Karolyi

"The biggest challenge for me was coming to the United States during the communist regime. I defected in 1980. Coming here, finding myself, not knowing anybody, not knowing the language, not knowing the customs of American life, being in a very different environment put me in a position I had never experienced before. Suddenly you are trying to survive, desperate to survive. I struggled over a year but the greatest learning experience that came from this challenge was not giving up my dream. Fight if you have to. You have to fight during difficult times, you have to do whatever you have to do in order to survive, and at that time for me it was all about survival. But surviving means that it is a hard fight, that's not fun, that's not pleasure, that's not satisfaction but a fight necessary in order to survive. The language barrier was unbelievably difficult and I had to resort to menial jobs just to survive. Every day I had to repeat to myself, 'This is not forever. This is just for survival and . . . I am not going to die today.'

"After a very short time of two and half years I was able to produce America's first Olympic Gymnastic Champion. That was unbelievably satisfying. I conquered the mountain, I felt like I did yet, I did it through difficult circumstances.

"Remember, never to forget, what is your dream, what is your life, what is your beloved profession."

"Every day I had to repeat to myself, 'This is not forever. This is just for survival and . . . I am not going to die today.'"

—Bela Karolyi

Can you imagine yourself going to another country, directly after college, with no support from your parents, no money to get started, no place to stay, and no knowledge of the language? Add to that hiding from the government while you're escaping to the other country, and you can't even say good-bye to your family or tell them where you're going. I asked Bela what message he would like to share with young students today.

Courageous Journey

"This message is a real message, which I learned in my life. I learned at a very young age, of my dream and my personal drive to become somebody in the gymnastic and coaching area, I was never in between ideas of who I wanted to be. In my mind there was only one thing, my love and the love in my heart was directing me toward this activity. After all these years of looking back, my suggestion would be to do in your life what your heart is telling you to do. Do in your life what you love the most, do in your life what is most important, what you are most gifted at. Do something that you know you can put your heart into, something you can be strong at, something that will give you great satisfaction and will take you on a beautiful journey. A courageous journey of your life, if not, then spending your life in a profession that you don't like is a very dull and sad story. Just do it! Do what your heart is telling you to do and do what you are best at.

"Spending your life in a profession that you don't like is a very dull and sad story."

—Bela Karolyi

"I think to become successful you have to have the love and passion in the profession we are practicing. We lead by example. In my mind, success is never coming unless you put your heart into it."

Chapter 4

Time Management

Schedule Your Success

I have had the pleasure and honor of speaking to thousands of students over the past few years. I hand out a questionnaire to try to learn more about them and their challenges. Some of the responses are comical and some are direct from the heart. One thing I ask them to do is:

Write down three challenges you have today as a culinary student.

After compiling the first five hundred questionnaires, I learned that the top three challenges students say they face are:

Number 1:
   Time management
Number 2:
   Finding a good job after graduation
Number 3:
   Finances

That time management is identified as the top challenge by most students certainly took me by surprise. I thought finances would be number one. When I read all of the questionnaires, I could almost hear the desperate tones in their voices.

This chapter is one of the first in the book to emphasize just how important it is for you to manage your time wisely and effectively if you are going to be successful, whether in school or your first job. And I'll share with you a secret: Time management does not get any easier as time passes, so it's best to start on your time management skills now.

> I'll share with you a secret: Time management does not get any easier as time passes.

Balance of Scheduling

I cannot emphasize enough the importance of a schedule. The art and skill of scheduling will have a direct impact on your work ethic and work habits, and thus your success. Proper scheduling can make the difference between doubling your output of work or losing days' and weeks' worth of valuable time. As you know, once that time is gone, it's gone; you're not getting it back. All we can do is look forward and try to do better tomorrow. Nor does it matter what kind of work it is. Whether you are in school, are experiencing your first year on the job, or have twenty years as an executive chef, scheduling will be one of the most effective tools you can master.

CALENDAR

Let's start with the calendar. I did not take full advantage of proper scheduling techniques until later in my career. For years I wasted valuable time during the day. Many days I could only accomplish one item on my to-do list at work. There is nothing more annoying than seeing your list pile up in front of you and only knocking off one to-do item for every eight that you receive. You soon will be buried and frustrated. The sooner you learn great scheduling practices, the quicker you will become more successful and effective.

> The sooner you learn great scheduling practices, the quicker you will become more successful.

For years I could not remember everything I needed to be doing, so I started writing everything down. Next thing I knew, my only accomplishment was a pile of lists; no or little actual work was getting done. Now I print out my calendar from the computer and schedule all my projects on it. This is where the success or failure variable comes in. I look at my calendar as a contract. You have to make a pact with yourself. Everything you put in your calendar YOU DO! Period. It's also crucial to be honest with yourself and be realistic about your calendar and what is a reasonable amount to accomplish. It's important not to overload your calendar or set yourself up for failure. At the same time, push yourself to be successful and accomplish more.

Sometimes I schedule myself heavily with commitments, speaking engagements, and demonstrations, as well as all my work responsibilities. I do this to push myself, force myself to stay sharp and committed. It's important to keep yourself motivated and on your toes. Commit yourself to study and take advantage of all of your time. You don't want to look back on time wasted with regret, wishing that you had used your time better. Spend time in your school's library (yes, there is one!) and take advantage of all the videos and reference books they have. Challenge yourself to learn outside of your work station.

It's also important to use the right medium as your calendar. It doesn't matter if you create a calendar in a notebook or use a monthly calendar that hangs on your wall, your mobile phone calendar application, the calendar function that's part of your computer operating system, or any other calendar form. Use one that works for you and that you can access daily on a regular basis.

So organize your time and schedule yourself wisely, and whatever you put in your schedule becomes your contract and your word. Go for it, just do it, schedule it and hold yourself accountable.

> Whatever you put in your schedule becomes your contract and your word.

SCHEDULE YOUR SUCCESS!

At one point in my life, I had so many to-do notes on my desk that my head was spinning. I was trying to write notes to be organized, and with all the disorganization on my desk, I was more confused than ever. I would begin to feel overwhelmed and sometimes panic. There were days I missed a lot of time because I was not organized at all. So I want to share one concept that I learned from Coach Lou Holtz, the famous football coach from Notre Dame. I had the distinct pleasure of hearing Coach Lou Holtz speak at River Oaks Country Club at a party for one of the members. Knowing everything in the kitchen was running smoothly, I sneaked in the back of the party room, next to the audiovisual guy, so I could hear. (Little secret here: Chefs have a great advantage because we have all the food. If you want the best seat in the house, feed the AV guy!)

Coach Holtz said many things that touched me that day, but the one that stuck with me was what he calls the WIN theory. WIN stands for "What's Important Now?" Doesn't this put everything into perspective? When feeling overwhelmed in anything or everything, just stop, take a deep breath, and figure out "What's Important Now"! On any given day I may have twenty to thirty to-do items on my list. Using the WIN theory helps take all the anxiety out of the process by making me determine what the priorities are. Figure out "what's important now," and act on it.

"WIN: What's Important NOW?"

Coach Lou Holtz

SCHEDULING

Study time, school time, work time, family time, and play/hobby time are possibly some of the time management frustrations you may be experiencing. Making time for all of these is part of maintaining a balanced work and private life, and all should be treated seriously.

Play Time

Many times I see that people do not schedule their play time. For years I never scheduled my vacation time, thinking that I would take time off when the business slowed down. Finally after a few years I got a little smarter and started to schedule some time off. I am still guilty of not properly scheduling quality family time.

Time away from work or school or anything that requires some sort of responsibility is important. You need to refresh and recharge. If you don't, you will never really operate at 100 percent of your capability, or at least not for long. Play time will mean many things to many people. It may be dining out with a friend; playing with loved ones; going to sporting events, movies, or shows; going to a park; working out; or simply staying home and surfing the Internet. However you define play time, make sure to schedule for it.

You can get "double points" if you have a hobby that also benefits your professional knowledge or your career. I try to save all my trade journals and magazines and schedule a time on Saturday mornings to catch up on them. It is a little quieter time and it helps me stay current with industry trends and practices.

If your hobby helps you physically and mentally, you are going to be much happier in life. I like to give exercise its own scheduled time because I believe it is that important, but some of you may find it easier to schedule it as part of your play or hobby time. NEVER do nothing! Remember, just do something! So schedule something with a friend or loved one. Or maybe you like to take time to be quiet and by yourself, and that is OK, too. Just be sure to schedule this decompression time. It will charge you back up for your professional work.

> NEVER do nothing.

EXERCISE AND WORKOUT TIME

Find that one thing that clears your head and gives you energy, and Just Do It! For me, that is an invigorating workout. We are all in the hospitality field, and a big part of our responsibility is to feed people. Two important factors can contribute to the poor health of employees or chefs in the hospitality field: the fact that we are constantly around food and need to taste everything, and our schedule. Early mornings, late nights, weekends, and holidays don't always lend themselves to spare time, let alone time to work out. It's all about scheduling it.

We all need a release. I believe chefs have an awesome responsibility not only to care for the ones they feed but to practice a healthy lifestyle themselves. Chefs are constantly around food, so we have to be careful of our environment and schedule. If you need exercise, fight for it and schedule it.

Work Time

It is our work or school time that takes up most of our days. In most cases, we do not schedule work, work schedules us. So how do we fit this into our schedule, or at least control it? I have some steps that may help. And remember, your work ethic will dictate your success.

> Your work ethic will dictate your success.

1. A Chef Who Is Vested in You

One of the top questions I get is: "How do I secure a good job while still in school?" Because almost any job you receive once you finish school will not make you rich, the most important thing to remember is to get a job that will provide an outstanding learning opportunity. A tool that may help you is a "sit down" with a chef at school or your externship (or both). Remember, you have to schedule this appointment with your chef. He or she is a very busy person. Chefs have a schedule too. Be sure to explain the purpose for this sit down. This will give the chef time to think about the meeting as well as give you time to line up all your questions and review what it is you want to go over with him or her.

> Get a job that will provide an outstanding learning opportunity.

At your meeting, share your goals so the chef becomes vested in your future. Share your road map to success so he or she can help you define it, refine it, and, ultimately, achieve it. Gain the chef's support to help you excel in whatever you want to do, both in school and in the workplace. With other professionals vested in your future and education, your chances of success will be higher. The secret now is that they want you to succeed.

I love helping chefs and student interns be successful in school. It took me a while to get good at this. I was so busy in my daily routines that I found myself never doing anything to help the success of those in my kitchen just starting out in this industry. Then one day, many years ago, a student came to me asking for help with his practical exam. He was very nervous about the test. So I asked him for all the guidelines, and we set up a virtual test where he practiced and three sous chefs and I judged. After he ran through the program three times, with the sous chefs standing over him correcting his every move, the student was confident about the test. So now we make it a point to be sure all of our students are ready for their practicals. This is a win-win situation for the student and the chef. The student does well in school, and the chef can be proud that he or she has helped a young person.

But the ultimate success in this depends on your work ethic and work habits. You need to back up your goals and plan for success with hard work and extra effort. The chef will not bend over backward for you if you don't follow through. This means volunteering for special events, helping whenever possible, being as flexible as you can. If your work ethic is above and beyond all expectations, your chef-mentor will work hard for you.

2. School Time

Just like work time, school time is relatively predetermined for you. Some schools have morning and afternoon classes (and sometimes night classes). Many times you are able to request which session you want to be in. You may want to give some particular thought as to which shift allows you the most flexibility with the rest of your schedule. If you are working, is it easier for you to work one particular shift over the other? One thing about working a day shift is that there is a better chance of getting out of work by a specific time. When you work a P.M. shift, many times you have no idea when you are getting out, because it is based on the business at hand.

Some schools have a standard block form, meaning that once you start school your schedule is pretty much set until you graduate. In this case you do not have much of a choice and need to follow the schedule the school has for you. Think of it as one less schedule you need to worry about, and focus instead on the other schedules in your life.

Other schools have more flexibility and allow you to pick your classes as you go. These schools are a little easier when it comes to scheduling the rest of your responsibilities and work, but in this environment you have to be incredibly focused. The fact that your school schedule in not already predetermined means it is up to you to set, organize, and maintain your school schedule. You should seek some advice from the school and a department advisor to be sure your thought process makes sense.

In many cases, my property works around the student's schedule, and vice versa. Remember, what goes around comes around! What I mean is, there are some properties that do not have the flexibility to simply work you when you are available, so it may be up to you to carefully schedule your classes around your work, if working while in school is a must. It is a give and take relationship. Hopefully the chef will do his or her best to work around your schedule, and you have to do your best to work around the business at hand. Respect your boss and the job. Most importantly, schedule a sit down with the chef well in advance of scheduling the next quarter of school. Do not wait until the last minute. If you do, you may find yourself being forced into whatever classes are left, which will dictate what your work schedule can be. And this may not coincide with what is needed of you at work. If you plan your time and schedule appropriately, you won't be forced to choose between school and work; you can accommodate both.

If you're proactive and plan your next quarter well in advance, you will most likely get the classes you want, and a schedule that coincides with your work, and everyone will be happy. Your chef will appreciate your honesty and the fact that you're mature enough to schedule well in advance.

ADVICE FROM CULINARY EDUCATORS

Q: *What are the most common mistakes you see students making?*

A: Students, and many people in general, often don't believe in their ability to achieve their own dreams. And, frequently, they don't reach high enough to begin with. Most goals can be achieved through conscious effort, discipline, and tenacity. The difference between successful students, accomplished chefs, winning culinary competitors, and prosperous entrepreneurs compared to the rest, is their dogged desire to be great and the willingness to dedicate the requisite time and effort to be great. Study, practice, research . . . immerse yourself in the subject until it becomes clear and comfortable in your mind. Match high aspirations with high energy, and the world is your banquet.

Robert Garlough

A: In cooking I would say that there are some simple [rules] that are commonly overlooked:

   i. Flavor comes from caramelization
  ii. Taste as you cook
 iii. Make sure your knives are sharp
 iv. Work clean and organized—take an extra moment to stay that way
  v. Follow basic procedures exactly
 vi. Know that a recipe is a guide; build your flavor memory so that you can adjust based on the quality of raw materials

Paul Sorgule, CEC, AAC

A: Students underestimate the importance of working in the industry they are studying to join. Most college students also miss the opportunity to participate in or volunteer for community functions that are relevant to their studies; such activities enhance leadership/soft skills, which are beneficial to building a résumé or portfolio. Lack of time management skills hinders homework assignments, study time, projects, and networking opportunities for most college students—not only hospitality students.

Kirk T. Bachmann

A: Underestimating the change that is demanded from the hospitality industry. It is a lifestyle switch: the unsociable hours, high-pressure environment, and modest pay, especially at the beginning, and, of course, at times trying to keep up with the pace and enjoying a life outside of work.

Dr. William Gallagher, H.C.
Past President of the World Association of Chefs Society (WACS)

A: Students today are entering a very competitive job market. They must prepare to work harder than others to advance or realize promotion. Be the hardest worker out there. Sweat equity.

This has been a not-so-secret element of success forever. Whoever works the hardest and bellyaches the least, usually will get the job.

Students should also develop an understanding that a job requires that you should work toward meeting the needs of the company. That's why they give you that thing called a check every week or two. Find out the company mission statement and make a contribution to help fulfill it.

Daniel Hugelier, CMC

3. Study Time

Study time should be easy. By now you know the rest of your schedule, so figure out what time is left. Try to schedule a time and a place that is conducive to great study habits. Your school library or a quiet room with great lighting usually is the best. It should be someplace where you can stay focused and that has few distractions. Set yourself up for success. Try to schedule this time when you are feeling fresh or refreshed.

> Schedule a time and place that is conducive to great work habits.

Do not take the attitude of doing schoolwork just for the sake of doing it. You are doing it to get ahead. Work at it with meaning and diligence. Remember, you get out of it what you put into it. Carefully find and schedule this time and be consistent with your studies. You will be rewarded not only during school but when you are in your workplace.

My assistant has a very full schedule. She works forty hours a week and goes to school full time. I asked her how she manages to study effectively. She made a brilliant comment. She said the best time to study is directly after school. Meaning, when you get out of class, this is the best time to reflect and study on the subject, while it is fresh in your mind. I believe this makes perfect sense. At the same time, you should discipline yourself to study one hour before your class, to review. This is especially important if you have a particular class once a week.

4. Family Time

Lastly we have family time. It is difficult to balance work and school and family life. I speak to you from experience, not as an expert on this topic. I am always being asked, "How do you balance your life, your work, the Culinary Olympic teams, and your family?" The answer is I'm not sure I do. Many times it manages me. My schedules are usually very tight and in line. One thing is for sure, the only reason my family understands is that I take time to share with them what I am doing. I take them on as many trips with me as possible.

> Family Time. I speak to you from experience, not as an expert on this topic.

Share what you're doing with those important in your life right now. Share with them your schedule and what you are doing, where you are going, what your goals are, and what your day is like, so they can be vested in *YOU*. Just as important as having a chef vested in you, you need to get those closest to you to *believe* in who you are and what you are doing.

When I was on the New England Culinary Olympic team, I was the executive sous chef at the Balsams Grand Resort Hotel in Dixville Notch, New Hampshire. When I was getting ready for a practice session, this was my schedule:

Work a normal sixty-hour work week for the resort.

Work another forty hours preparing for the practice session, working some nights until midnight or 2:00 A.M.

I would not have any days off leading up to the session. Friday night I would finish around midnight, go home, and lie down until 2:00 A.M. Then I would wake up, pack my food, and drive four hours to Boston to catch a flight to Orlando, Florida, by 7:00 A.M. I would arrive in Orlando at 11:00 A.M., go directly to Disney World, which was our practice facility, and work to 1:00 A.M. Sunday morning I was up at 6:00 A.M. and worked until 1:00 A.M. I was up again Monday morning at 6:00 A.M. and worked until 6:00 P.M., then packed up, rushed off to the airport—many times still in my chef whites and smelling like smoked salmon—and jumped on a flight back to Boston. I would arrive around midnight, try my best to stay awake and drive four hours back to The Balsams to arrive by 5:00 A.M. I might stop several times to do jumping jacks or jog around the car in the freezing cold to try to stay awake. This left me just enough time to get home, shower, and arrive at work on time—never late—at 6:30 in the morning.

Now all my staff knew was that I was off, missing all the busy times at the resort. They had to bust their butts while I was in Disney World. They would ask, "How was your vacation at Disney World?"

This was tough to swallow after all the hard work I went through. So the moral of the story is: "You've got to share." You have to be sure your staff knows what you are doing and what you're working toward. If you bring back recipes, videos, pictures, or anything that will share your experience with those you work with, they will support you. They will be hungry for more. They will help you get ready. They want to learn and be a part of your success, so reel them in. Everyone benefits from this education, and next thing you know they will be backing you up and watching your back.

I have prepared a sample schedule for a calendar week for a student and an entry-level cook. The purpose of these examples is to inspire you with some possible scheduling ideas. There is no way I can tell you perfectly how to schedule yourself; that is for you to decide. Every individual has different needs and circumstances. My goal is to simply point out some concepts I believe are important. If you make a contract with yourself, if you make a pact with yourself, that when you put something in your schedule you do it to the best of your abilities, you will be more successful. So use these examples as a template for your path to success. If you're like me, you'll find it will help tremendously. It has been one of my biggest secrets.

Example of a Schedule: Entry-Level Cook

Sunday	Monday	Tuesday	Wednesday	Thursday	Friday	Saturday
OFF	OFF	Work 2–10 P.M.	Work 2–10 P.M.	Work 2–10 P.M.	Work 2–10 P.M.	Work 2–10 P.M.
• Eat breakfast/read newspaper	• Eat breakfast/read newspaper	• 7–7:45 A.M.	• 7–7:45 A.M.	• 7–7:45 A.M.	• 7–7:45 A.M.	• 7–7:45 A.M.
• Call a family member	• 8–9:30 A.M. Workout/Gym	• Eat breakfast/read newspaper	• Eat breakfast/read newspaper	• Eat breakfast/read newspaper	• Eat breakfast/read newspaper	• Eat breakfast/read newspaper
• Personal errands	• Plan something completely fun	• 8–9:30 A.M. Hobby time	• 8–9:30 A.M. Workout/Gym	• 8–10 A.M. Professional growth time	• 8–9:30 A.M. Workout/Gym	• 10–11 A.M. Read trade journals
• Dinner/share time with loved one, communicate						• 12 P.M. House chores
						• After work play with colleagues

Example of a Schedule: Full-Time Student

Sunday	Monday	Tuesday	Wednesday	Thursday	Friday	Saturday
OFF						
• Sleep in/ have breakfast	• 5:15 A.M. Have breakfast	• 8 A.M. Eat breakfast	• 5:15 A.M. Have breakfast	• 8 A.M. Eat breakfast	• 7 A.M. Eat breakfast	• 8 A.M. Eat breakfast
• Call a loved one	• 6–11:30 A.M. Culinary lab	• 9–11 A.M. Workout/Gym	• 6–11:30 A.M. Culinary lab	• 9–11 A.M. Workout/Gym	• 8 A.M.–12 P.M. Class	• 9–11:30 A.M. Homework
• Volunteer somewhere culinary related	• 12–12:30 P.M. Sit down with instructor	• Class 3–6 P.M.	• 12–12:30 P.M. Sit down with instructor	• 2–10 P.M. Work	• 12 P.M.–1 P.M. Go to library	• 2–10 P.M. Work
	• 1 P.M. Do homework	• 7 P.M. Do homework	• 1 P.M. Do homework		• 1–4 P.M. Do homework	• Meet with friends after work, fun time
	• Do something completely fun				• 5:30–9:30 P.M. Culinary lab	

Spend Time with a Loved One; Share Your Day

Take a look at the cook's schedule (p. 50) carefully. I want to point out a few important things.

Breakfast

Notice that I put eat breakfast on both student and cook schedule. Eat breakfast! I understand that we will not "schedule eating," but I want to make a point here. Too many times I see chefs, cooks, and students skipping what I, and many others, believe is the most important meal of the day. In the hospitality field, our work day is already demanding; to me, the most important thing you can do is wake up in time to gather your thoughts for the day and have a good breakfast. You will work better with nourishment and a proper diet first thing in the morning. You will find that you will be much more alert for the day, that you have given some thought to the tasks you have ahead of you, that you have more energy, and most importantly, that you are more productive.

Read What Your Boss Reads

Pay attention to all your surroundings. Part of your responsibilities while growing up and into your culinary career is to keep your eyes wide open and see as much as possible. In Chapter Two, I outlined how to research the top four professionals who do what you want to do. I did not ask you to research them for the sake of researching them; I want you to live through them. I asked you to study their business model because we both know it worked for them. We know they became successful, so it worked for them. So why not do what they did?

I want you to read what your boss reads. Pay close attention to what your boss or bosses do every day. Many times we get too caught up in the simple task in front of us, and we don't see what is going on around us. Imagine if you paid attention to everything your boss did, if you studied his or her every move. How does your boss talk to the GM, to the guests? How does your boss dress? When does your boss come to work and leave work? How does your boss instruct the staff? And finally, how does he or she cook? Your boss is the one leading the team. Technically this is the most skilled and best-trained person for the job. If you watch his or her every move, good or bad, you are bound to learn. You don't have to wait until you're a chef to read the periodicals your boss reads, you can start now. You don't have to wait until you're a chef to talk to the guests the way your boss does—you can start now. You get the idea. You need to have your eyes peeled wide open! The first clue here is that you need to care about what is going on around you, and that takes effort. It is so much easier not to care and just peel the bag of carrots in front of you. It actually takes effort and energy to care what people are doing around you. So what this means is that if you do your job with a sense of urgency, while paying close attention to what other people around you are doing, you will learn that much more. I call this kitchen coordination.

You need to care about what is going on around you.

Communicate and Share Time

In the schedule given previously, the cook is off on Sunday and Monday. One of the most difficult things to do in our business is to have a meal with our family or friends, because we are normally working and preparing meals for everyone else. Be sure you schedule time and meals with the people you care about. Insist on it. Don't let this get away from you. If you practice early on the importance of eating with family, you will take it with you throughout your career.

Communication sometimes becomes scarce because chefs can come home late at night. Family may be in bed already, or the chefs may be too tired or brain-dead to carry on a conversation. Be sure to share your day as much as possible with your family so they understand what you're going through and can be a part of your life in some way.

Your Own Time

Find time for yourself to do something that interests you outside of your profession. Whether it's working out, taking on a hobby, reading a good book, or anything else, having personal time is one more step in the process of rejuvenating yourself on a regular basis.

Professional Growth Time

It is vitally important that you take advantage of as much free time as possible. Meaning that if you can focus on your career, and spend spare time working toward your personal growth in your profession, you will obviously be better off. Again, it is so easy to do nothing. If you can plan time in your schedule for your own professional growth, you will quickly set yourself apart from others. Personal growth in your profession could be studying classical or contemporary recipes, researching on the computer, Googling other famous chefs to learn more about their success, going to chef association meetings and clubs, and, of course, volunteering.

Volunteer As Much As Possible

As I advised before, don't let great opportunities pass you by. Those who volunteer will soon be recognized as special individuals. You will get opportunities to network with special individuals who care about what they do. If you volunteer, you will find more doors opening for you, more opportunities, and you will create very special relationships that are priceless. The education you receive from volunteer opportunities is beyond words.

Your Game Plan

What's your game plan? Add the following items to the game plan you are creating for yourself.

- Start using a calendar as an organizational tool. Whether it's electronic or paper, put everything in the calendar and treat it like a contract. Be true to it and honest with yourself. The first step in effective time management is to know what your schedule is and when your tasks need to be completed.

- Find at least one hour during this week for personal time, whether it's spending time with family and friends, alone time, or just plain goofing off.

Chapter Lessons

So here's what you need to do to begin establishing effective time management skills:

- Look at your calendar of to-do lists and appointments, and view them as a contract.

- Figure out WIN: "What Is Important Now?"!

- Schedule your success.

- Schedule work time, play time, family time, school time, and study time.

- Schedule a sit down with a chef-mentor, and gain his or her vested interest in you.

- Help yourself first, or don't complain about it.

- Share your goals and expectations with those closest to you. Gain their support so they have a vested interest in you.

CHEF SAM CHOY

Aloha

Chef Sam Choy is one of the nicest and warmest people you will ever meet. It's an added bonus that he is one of the most respected chefs in our industry. He is an award-winning restaurateur, best-selling cookbook author, and TV host. Sam educates people the world over about the wonderful, diverse cultures and flavors that converge in Hawaii. He opened his first restaurant in 1981 on the Big Island of Hawaii

Sam Choy

and now owns and operates two restaurants in Honolulu, one in Guam, and seven in Japan. Sam is basically a self-made man who grew up in a time when local chefs in Hawaii were not considered celebrities, and the cuisine was not celebrated.

Keep Grinding

Sam told me, "Many years ago, when the hospitality field was just starting to boom, a lot of the hotels in Hawaii that had European general managers were also hiring European chefs. For me, being a product of the Islands, I never changed the way I cooked. I always did it the way my mom and dad taught in the kitchen at home. I have always stayed true to my beliefs and kept grinding and grinding. That was a tough time for me, cooking the way I was taught and constantly being told by chefs who were not local that my way was incorrect. So, I did my best to create a style that was the best of both worlds. I never gave up, I never changed my cooking style, and now I get invited almost daily, to cook all over the world."

Sam has a philosophy that fits his personality. He is very passionate not only about food, but also about the way it is grown, which carries over to his philosophy on life and how we should work.

"When the going gets tough, that's when you need to get back to the basics. That's what I always preach, and I believe is the real key to our profession. Plant a seed and watch it, nourish it, then you can enjoy the fruits of your hard work. Be persistent, and be very, very, very passionate about what you do. That's what I always tell the young generation, that no matter how frustrating it gets in the food industry, if you have a good structure, you'll never ever feel like you were left out. If you planted that seed in your education, and you work hard and take care of that seed, it will give you a great foundation to your success. You can't eat a tomato without planting a seed first. You can't be successful in our profession or any profession unless you learn the basics, plant those seeds, carefully craft your education and you will flourish."

Sam keeps it pretty simple, don't you think? And it makes perfect sense. You can't eat great-tasting fruit unless you plant the seeds first. You can't jump to the top of the ladder and expect to be the boss, or expect to get the big paychecks or the big promotions, unless your foundation has been properly laid. All champions have their own analogies of how to earn greatness and success, but it all boils down to how much time you spend on the details of your foundation.

Confidence

Sam talked to me a lot about confidence. "It's like a golfer leaning over a putt, and saying I can't make this. As soon as you think like this, you are done. So when the going gets tough, you breeze right through it, because you've got your foundation laid. You know how to deal with yourself, mentally, physically, and emotionally. You will succeed because you prepared and did your homework.

"I learned this from my parents: work smart and work hard. But in our industry you have to do both simultaneously. Because our business is very demanding and we are only as good as the last meal we put out. Keep it simple and bear down."

> *"Keep it simple and bear down."*
> —Chef Sam Choy

I like what Chef Choy says here: "bear down." You have to stay focused and keep at it. Stay with it, and remember what Chef John Folse said: Stickability. Stick with it and bear down.

Sam also talked with me about some of his early industry experiences and how they informed his philosophies. "I worked for Hilton and Hyatt, and I was very instrumental in a lot of the openings. I watched a lot of these corporate chefs work their hearts out, and at the end of their careers they get let go, given a watch, and told thank you. That's what got me fascinated. Do I want to do this for the rest of my life or do I want to make something happen? I watched some of the most talented corporate chefs and hospitality people, at the end of their career, they were let go.

"I learned that when you are given an opportunity you take advantage of it. Just make something happen, that is where I have been my strongest. You can sit there, moan, cry, and regret, but why? Someone always has it worse; turn it around, make it happen. Be positive. You got to dig down deep and make it work. And that's what really turned me around. I made the decision to bear down and that is what I did."

"Just make something happen, that is where I have been my strongest."
—Chef Sam Choy

I asked Sam how he manages so many restaurants in so many places.

"You take it one meal at a time. It's work ethic; you got to make sure that all your people are buying into the same idea. I still cook as passionately as I did twenty years ago. If I had to do one thing over again, I would say that I wish I was a better listener. You have to be very passionate about what you do or you will not survive."

Chapter 5

Choosing Your Externship

Keep Chewing

For some of you, an externship will be your first real job in your chosen profession. Looking for a job will always be a nervous time in your life, whether it is your first job or a job change midway through your career.

While in school, attend ALL job fairs the school may have—and I mean ALL. I don't care if you have been in school only for a week, or if you're graduating next week and think you have already signed on to your dream job. You need to be knowledgeable about everything that is out there, so go to all of them. It's never too early to make contacts. Interview as much as possible, even if it's only an informational interview. The more you interview, the more comfortable you will feel and the more experienced you will become. This is crucially important, especially later in life when you are going for that big job, and your body language and nervousness could keep the employer from seeing the real you.

> The more you interview, the more comfortable you will feel and the more experienced you will become.

First Impressions

First impressions are often the truest. You never get a second chance at a first impression. You have to look and act like a professional if you want to be taken seriously. Imagine what an employer will think if you can't even look like a professional during the interview. Chances are, if you do not have the discipline to look like a professional for an important interview, you will not look professional on a daily basis. If you do not have a suit, dress in professional attire, wear a clean and crisp chef uniform. And I mean complete uniform: tie, apron, and name tag if applicable. There are likely many chefs also applying for the position for which you are interviewing. All it takes is one reason for an employer not to hire you. Don't give them that reason.

> First impressions are often the truest.

When I was in culinary school, I had an externship all planned overseas in London, England. All systems were go until one month prior, when the deal fell through because the property decided to put a hiring freeze into effect during the time I was to go. Prior to the hiring freeze, there had been a job fair at the school. I attended, but did not take it very seriously because I thought I already had a job, so I went in casual clothes. I did interview halfheartedly with a couple of companies, for the experience, but I already had my sights set on England. Well, after the deal fell through, I started calling these companies frantically to try to get a job. One of the chefs who interviewed me said he actually was very interested in me but wanted to know why I did not dress appropriately for the interview. I told him my story, and his response was, "So now you're desperate. You should not put all your eggs into one basket, chef." He went on to lecture me that if you decide to do something as important as interviewing for a job, you do it professionally and not halfway. Who knows when you may cross paths with that interviewer again? Our industry may be large, but in many ways it is small. I agreed with him and apologized, and he hired me. I know I got lucky.

Moral of the story: You just never know. You may already have your dream job, you may have a signed offer for a job, or maybe a company decides to back out at the last minute. So whatever you do, do it with 100 percent of your efforts or don't do it at all.

Sit-Down Sessions

One exercise you should take full advantage of is what I call *sit downs*. While you're going to school, be sure to talk to as many of your instructors as possible. Take advantage of the experts who are in front of you NOW! Make it a point to have a sit down with each of your instructors at least once, sometime during the term of your course or just after the class is complete and before you move on to the next.

> "You can't stay in your corner of the forest waiting for others to come to you. You have to go to them sometimes."
>
> —Winnie the Pooh

Make an appointment with them so you can pick their brains. Have your list of questions *ready*. You want to learn as much from them as possible. Here are some questions you may ask your instructors.

- How did you get started in the culinary field?
- What jobs have you held?
- What was your best culinary work experience?
- What was your worst culinary work experience?
- If you could change one thing about your culinary education, what would it be?
- Have you received any awards?
- Who was your mentor, or who had the biggest influence on your career?
- How would you evaluate my work in class?
- What could I have done better?
- What do you see as my challenges?
- What do you see as my strengths?
- What kind of job do you think I would be good at?
- Ask their opinions of the road you are thinking of taking.

You get the idea. You can come up with your own questions, and you should. The important thing is that you take advantage of the talented chef in front of you. Take advantage of the opportunity to learn from the career he or she has had. In turn, your instructors may have some contacts that may help you. If you worked your tail off in class and volunteered every chance you got, the instructor will be happy to give you a letter of reference and take an interest in your externship as well as your post-school career.

Educational Diary

Keep a "diary" of sit-down sessions. Can you imagine the wealth of knowledge you would have after your school year if you had a sit down with every instructor you came in contact with? The additional lessons that you will learn in these personal sessions will be worth your time. You will gain great advice from a wide variety of experiences, and it will not cost you more than your time and some focus. As an added benefit, your instructor will realize that you are very serious about your career. You will stand out; at the same time, you will grow as a culinarian.

Go to school READY. Think about your day before you get there, as we discussed in Chapter 4. Think about what questions you can ask your instructors. They do not necessarily have to be about the class. You can ask about the chef, or about what you read the night before. Pick the brains of all your chefs *every* day! Constantly visit with your chefs to the point where they will almost expect you to stop by and say hello. And don't just cultivate the chef you have for the class now; continue the relationship with your instructors all through school. Gain the reputation of wanting to learn every day. A fantastic exercise for you in this respect can be as follows:

Every time you meet a new professional, a new chef, a new acquaintance, anyone, quickly think of a question you can ask that you will learn something from. It may be something about the state this person is from, what that region is known for, any piece of information that will make you more knowledgeable than you were before you met him or her. This exercise will actually make you remember a new acquaintance's name better, as well. It's also a great avenue for follow-up in the future. If you want to contact someone in the future, it's always great to remind him or her of the conversation, however brief, the two of you had. This goes both ways. It helps you remember details about this person, but it might also help jog his or her memory of having met you.

Set Your Goals and Maximize Your First Growth

Your externship will be the first soul-searching exercise in your career with regard to "What am I doing, where am I going, and how am I going to get there?" The most important thing you should always remember, wherever you go, is:

Search out the best experience you can find.
Search out the people and places with the best reputation.
Search for a mentor.

Before starting your first job or externship, define what it is you want to accomplish in your time on the job. What are your expectations, and how will you achieve those goals?

Do not take a job just out of convenience or because it pays more. The first jobs of your career will be the most important ones of your life. The early years of your education and training set the pace for your career.

They are the building blocks and foundation of your skills. The older you get and the higher up the ladder you climb, the more you are expected to know the answers. So enjoy being the student now. Don't be afraid to ask all the questions you need answered, because one day you will be the person answering the questions.

> If you want to be an average employee with average wages and an average lifestyle, just do the minimum.

While on your externship, you have a few basic requirements for your school to complete during the course of your work. These requirements are important but just the bare minimum of what you should be working on. Don't get caught "just getting by." If you want to be an average employee with average wages and an average lifestyle, just do the minimum.

Your externship or first job is a very important experience for you. This experience should be a burst to your confidence. I normally see new culinarians grow after this experience. Your first test in the market usually takes some of the greenness off you. It is important that you make the best out of this experience so you can maximize your growth from it.

When I was chef of the Balsams Grand Resort Hotel in Dixville Notch, New Hampshire, we had our apprentices go on externships six times during their three-and-a-half-year program. I tell you, when they graduated, these culinarians had a fantastic background of experience and traveling skills. It was amazing to see them grow from their first season, when they were not even sure how to set up their cutting board and knives to begin work, to finishing their senior year supervising stations. I love to see this growth more than anything in the world.

Now this will be the first job to which you can actually apply the following lessons. These lessons can become the first three goals you set for yourself.

Lesson #1

Get to know the job better than the person teaching you.

Lesson #2

Possess uncompromising levels of follow-through.

Lesson #3

Complete each task above and beyond all expectations.

Now this is the deal. You are in your first work environment. You have an opportunity to use some of the tools you have learned from your education and from this book to help you excel. Please be humble. Don't try to be a know-it-all right out of the gate. You will not impress anyone, trust me. Enjoy being a student. At this time in your life, it is not your job to try to out-cook the chef or the sous chef who is training you. It is your job to absorb everything you possibly can, good or bad. Yes, that is right: good or bad. All the lessons will be great lessons, even if they are bad ones. If you are able to learn from the bad ones, you will be educated all the more. You will be able to recognize the bad situation and be sure it never happens again, not under your watch. Just as important, you will learn how to get yourself out of a bad situation. So be humble, and respect all the employees at the facility, from the head chef to the dishwashers. Respect them in the way you wish to be respected.

> "When you're curious, you find lots of interesting things to do."
>
> —Walt Disney

I assume you will see a few different stations at your externship job. At the very least, you should work two different stations, and if you're lucky you can experience three. Be sure you attack these stations. If one of the goals you set for yourself is to learn the station and skills better than the person training you, you will learn a lot.

Build Your Resources

Now is the time to start building your resources. Create and build a file or binder for every station you work. For instance, if the first station you work is the breakfast line, by the end of the experience, you should have a complete binder that will allow you to train anyone. The binder should have all the information, ratios, recipes, and formulas to properly run the station. Imagine that you are now the chef; the binder should be so complete that you can hand it to one of your sous chefs with the confidence that he or she will now be able to run the station. All the special recipes, and ratios to feed fifty, one hundred, two hundred, and three hundred people are in the binder. There are drawings and pictures of station setups. If you take this exercise seriously, you will be using this reference binder for years to come. How cool is that! Be sure to be complete. If there are specialty sweet breads, muffins, sticky buns, or croissants coming from the bakeshop, be sure you know those recipes and have them documented.

Imagine if you do this with every station you work, from now until you become a sous chef. What a great library of knowledge you will have. But don't stop once you become a sous chef. This is a practice you should continue and add to throughout your career. Your goal should be to collect all the experiences possible. The more the better. Even if your goal is not to become a pastry chef, you need experience in the bakeshop to gain the knowledge of what is needed, to be able to speak intelligently to the pastry staff. Not only that, but you may find yourself at a property that does not have a pastry team, and it will be up to you to provide desserts. Just think about how impressed the chef you are interviewing with will be if you come equipped with the knowledge to contribute.

Stealing Experiences

Stealing experiences is a bonus. If you're not currently stealing them, start now. By this I mean, while you're on externship, learn as much as possible. You know you will not get a chance to work every station at the property, so once or twice a week, go in early or stay late and work another station, off the clock. Yes, off the clock. Don't think about how you're not being paid, but how you're getting ahead. You also will gain the respect of those around you, and especially the chef. If you're doing it because you want to learn, everyone else can and should be behind you. I am not saying burn yourself out, work 120 hours a week; I am saying schedule time a couple of times a week and make this happen. Your two- or three-station externship just turned into five!

> Stealing experiences is a bonus.

What else does your externship property do well? Find it, seek it out, and get the experience. Butcher shop, saucier, banquets, fine dining, poolside, even front of the house would all be great experiences. Take advantage of the time you are at this property and start building your resources and your references. Start chewing that table!

> Don't think about how you're not being paid, but how you're getting ahead.

When I was an apprentice at the Balsams Grand Resort Hotel, I was chewing big time. I wanted it all. I carved ice every moment I could. I collected patterns and designs and carved every ice block that came into the building. I taught myself over the course of a year. I did not get paid for it, but the way I looked at it, they did not charge me for the ice, either. I worked all the stations I possibly could. At the time, I did not have it in my head specifically to learn the station better than the person teaching me, but I did have the mindset to want to be in charge when the station chef was off. I wanted that chef to trust me with his job, which meant that I had to learn the job and understand it as well as the station chef.

After five years of this mentality as well as completing culinary school, I was promoted to executive chef of this resort—with sixty employees—at the ripe young age of twenty-five. Now there were some individuals who thought I was not old enough or did not have enough experience. They may or may not have been right, but one thing is for sure: Nobody knew the job better than I did, and nobody was willing to work as hard at it as I was. I made sure of it. There was not one station in the kitchen that I could not instruct someone on. Sometimes you have to pretend to be something before you can become it. Work hard and you will be rewarded. Trust me when I say: People will notice.

> Sometimes you have to pretend to be something before you can become it.

KITCHEN COORDINATION

Kitchen coordination is a talent that allows an individual to see everything that is going on in the kitchen. And you cannot just acquire this skill. It takes time to master the skill of kitchen coordination. In some ways it is like being an air traffic controller. You need to know what is coming and going at all times. If you practice this skill at a young age, you will benefit from it in the long run.

> You need to know what is coming and going at all times.

I have seen P.M. sous chefs who were great cooks but had no idea what the soup tasted like that day. They would get all their work done and get the party out, but they would have no idea if the garde manger was OK and on time, or know what the vinaigrette tasted like. So what I want you to do is be aware of your surroundings. Care about what is going on around you. Care about what your colleague is making next to you. Care about what time the party goes out, or what recipe the person next to you is making. How does the best sauté chef set up his or her station? What does the broiler chef use for seasonal blends?

> "If the person you are talking to doesn't appear to be listening, be patient. It may simply be that he has a small piece of fluff in his ear."
>
> —Winnie the Pooh

If you are given a task for the banquet going out later in the day, be aware of the entire menu, not just what you're working on. Make it a goal of every meal you are working on, that you should have all the recipes available to you to do the event yourself. If you had to instruct some students or other chefs in the kitchen on how to put that menu out, make sure that you could. This means you have to pay attention to more than just the task you are working on. Keep a close eye on your boss. Do what he or she does. Read what the chef reads. How does he or she run the kitchen? Talk to the guests? Provide leadership to the staff? How does the chef organize all the timings of the banquets? Get the idea? Keep your eyes wide open. Learn more than just the job at hand. Learn what is going on around you. You will be a much more valuable employee if you do. You will be more valuable because you will know more about what is going on in the kitchen.

Kitchen Coordination Lessons

- Learn all recipes of the day that are being used, not just the one you are working on.
- Care about what your neighbor is working on at all times.
- Pay attention to all timing in the kitchen.
- Constantly monitor how your boss works, acts, corresponds, and communicates.
- Taste everything!
- Collect as many recipes as you can.
- Care about EVERYTHING!

You will have more knowledge than the Joey next to you who is only concerned with peeling his carrots with his orange hands.

> Learn more than just the job at hand. Learn what is going on around you.

TRAVELING SKILLS

As a young person or new culinarian, you may have a few opportunities to travel and see different areas of the United States. Be sure to take full advantage of this. When I was executive chef at the Balsams, our apprentices had awesome opportunities to go on externship a total of six times before they graduated. Imagine the priceless experiences they received seeing six different properties and working at the Resort over a period of three years. The apprenticeship also gave them great experiences in traveling, what I call traveling skills. It gave the apprentices a great sense of survival: how to get there, how to set up short-term housing, and how to get back. Traveling skills are valuable and are always a wonderful experience. My lesson to you here is: Be sure you take in the sights while you are in another part of the country. Be sure to take in some culture. Understand the area you are in. Be sure to tour the city you are in, learn the history, and learn the food of the region.

One reason I find this such an important skill and something to take advantage of is that I am guilty of not doing this. While I've had the benefit of traveling, I always worked and never truly understood the area I was in. I have been all over the world competing, and because of the nature of competition, rarely got a chance to see the world, only worked in the kitchens all hours of the night. It is a crime to compete in Switzerland and not even manage to learn about it. So be sure to learn about the areas you are working in; you will be a more rounded person for doing so.

Keep chewing!

Your Game Plan

What's your game plan? Add the following items to the game plan you are creating for yourself.

- Be aware of all the externships that are available. Don't wait until it is time for you to go to find a place. Be interested in the students on extern now. Learn from them. Visit the externship office and gain as much help and experience as possible from the people working there. They are there to help you. It is never too early to investigate where you want to go.

- Talk to your instructors and learn from them. Try to schedule a sit down with every instructor you have. The instructors will take a genuine interest in you because you have taken a genuine interest in yourself.

- Continue to build your resources while you're on your externship. The harder you work, the better the reference. You want to have access to the chef's entire Rolodex, and you do that by blowing him away with your work.

Chapter Lessons

- Attend ALL job fairs, whether you already have a job opportunity or not.
- Interview as much as possible.
- You never get a second chance at a first impression.
- Dress for success.
- Schedule a sit down with every instructor you have. Take full advantage of their talent and success.
- Keep a diary of mentoring sessions.
- Search out the best experiences you can find.
- Search out the people and places with the best reputation.
- Search for a mentor, not money.
- Build your resources.
- Steal as many work experiences as you possibly can.
- Read what your boss reads. Study what he or she does day in and day out.
- Care about everything that is going on around you.

CHEF NORMAN VAN AKEN

From Hot Tar to Hot Star

Norman Van Aken

I had the great fortune of working with Chef Norman Van Aken as guest chefs during a fundraiser at Chef John Folse's great White Oak Plantation. To cook side by side with an icon like Chef Norman is very special. One of the things I liked most about it is that his wife Janet and son Justin helped him. I watched carefully as they worked in unison.

Chef Norman is an incredibly successful chef. He is in high demand, traveling all over the country donating his time for friends, charities, and goodwill. His restaurant, Norman's, is a landmark in the Orlando Ritz-Carlton, and he currently has another restaurant under construction in Miami. Norman was the first published celebrity chef in Florida and has many stories to share with you. I asked Norman how he got started in the business.

Searching for What Fits

"When I was growing up, being a chef was not as glamorous as it appears today. It seems that there is so much pre-information that exists for a young person today. The culinary field was a field unknown to anybody growing up during my time. Nobody ever talked about being a chef.

"I began cooking, not ever dreaming of becoming a chef. My first job was as a hot tar roofer. I worked a series of jobs when I got out of high school that included working in a factory making glass, in a factory making picture frames, I worked in a factory packing books, as a house painter, concrete sprayer in Kansas, and worked peddling flowers on the streets of Honolulu, Hawaii, Florida, and Colorado.

"My last job before going into cooking, the hot tar roofing job, I got fired from. One hot day during a roofing job it started to pour. I was so excited that it was raining and I don't think the boss appreciated my rain dance, so that was the last day as a hot tar roofer.

"So I picked up the *Circular*, the area newspaper, and saw an ad for a short-order cook for $3.25 an hour; I went into the neighborhood diner and found myself for the first time actually liking the job. I had no idea what this job meant for me or where I was going with it. Then I worked for five or six years before I worked in a place that was serious. I mean a lot of places were serious: serious about making money, serious about their next day off, serious about getting drunk, or whatever, but this was the first place that people were serious about cooking and being a chef. This was 1971."

To me, Chef Norman is a very important part of this book because he has mentored so many young chefs today, including his relationship with celebrity chef Charlie Trotter. I asked him about some of his experiences working with young, hungry chefs.

Patience

"At Norman's Restaurant about nine years ago I was working with a lot of young men and women in the restaurant who were in their early twenties. All were competing with each other to succeed and many of them were frustrated with where they were at in their career. They did not have their first cookbook yet, they were not on television, or in any magazines or newspapers. They were frustrated that none of these great things had happened to them yet. This bothered me a bit so I went back to my computer, developed a graph on my life, and came back two days later and had a team meeting."

> *"Greatness and success take time."*
> —Chef Norman Van Aken

"I told them all I wanted them to understand greatness and success take time; [I told them] 'It takes more time than you're giving yourselves. I want you to be fired up and I want you to be hungry and learn, but you need to understand I cooked for five years before I made a beurre blanc. I did not know what a beurre blanc was.' I started spitting out numbers and my personal experience and time line in my life. I was thirty-eight before I did my first cookbook, I was forty-four before I owned my first restaurant. I wanted them to see that I did not just spring out of a magic box and become instantly successful at the age of twenty-four.

"I guess what I am trying to say is that I want them to be hungry. I want them to be successful and eager to learn, but that greatness and excellence takes time."

Learning from Your Bumps

Success does not grow on trees. As Chef Sam Choy says, you have to plant a seed, water it, nurture it, and watch it grow before you can harvest it and enjoy its fruits. Our careers are much like a plant. If you don't nurture it, you will not be able to harvest much. This is a very important point Chef Norman makes. Look at his personal time line and understand how long it took him to be successful. Chef Norman is a very passionate man who overcame many challenges.

"Students should understand that there are going to be challenges and setbacks along the way. The students are frustrated because they see the success stories on television and in magazines and wonder why it is not happening to them.

"There are going to be times when you have to pick yourself up off the canvas and do it again. If you are VERY fortunate you will take two steps forward and [only] one step back. It is important that young people today understand this. You're not the only person this has ever happened to, and you need to show the world you are made of sterner stuff."

> *"You're not the only person this has ever happened to, and you need to show the world you are made of sterner stuff."*
>
> —Chef Norman Van Aken

This is so true. I believe when you experience failure it will be OK, you will be able to make peace with it because you now understand it is only a bump in your road to success. This bump was put there for you to understand, this bump is a gift and a lesson that will ultimately contribute to your future success.

Sound Advice

I asked Chef Norman how recent graduates should look at life the first few years out of college and what their expectations of pay should be.

"I would tell them this: that I would be suspicious if they were getting paid a lot of money directly out of school. If I were you, young person, I would be suspicious if someone was offering you four or five dollars more an hour than the other places. Chances are if they are able to pay you all this money, they are probably taking shortcuts and you are not going to learn the craft. That money or the larger pay scale may not be the best education for you in the long run. I understand that you would be eager to pay back student loans, but you may find yourself after ten years not knowing nearly as much had you taken the job that offered you the great opportunity to learn the craft and a property that did not take the shortcuts."

Read and Learn

Chef Norman also talked with me about how important reading is. He says, "Another thing that just astonishes me is how few young people actually read. They spend so much money to go to school, and when they get out they just don't read. It is sad to me that the average graduate's attention span when it comes to reading is lacking, to say the least. At my restaurant, I built a small room with a table and two chairs which house[s] close to four hundred of my cookbook [collection]. I invited any of my people who worked in the restaurant to use this library, and it blew me away that none of them took advantage of it. I had a strong crew, and almost nobody took advantage of these resources. It astounds me that they don't expose their minds to these resources.

"And the other thing is they don't do enough stage work. It is crazy to me that students will be happy to pay forty, fifty, sixty thousand dollars to go to school but they won't spend an extra day working in one of the finer establishments in their state, their region, or in the country, learning from successful people. It kills me.

"My advice to young people would be to read. If you read you are learning, so read and find a successful chef or property and stage for a day or a week or a month. Invest in your own future."

I asked Chef Norman what one of the biggest lessons in his life was. There was a long pause before his answer.

"Well, that in life there is going to be pain. And my response to it is to try and remake the world, and find that place of happiness through food. My mom and dad had a difficult relationship and that was hard and rough on me in many ways. My dad died when I was seventeen. My response to that is that you can be crushed beneath the wheels of hard times or take those wheels and make them into something beautiful. Life is not worth living with a broken heart, you need to overcome it."

I then asked what the most devastating time in his life was. Again a long pause, then some laughter.

"God, I hope it has already happened and it's over with. I guess it would have to be the first time we went out of business, the first time we had to close our doors. We considered it our dream restaurant. I just had been published and going on tour with the book, [when] we had to close Mira (which means "look" in Spanish). We made some first-time errors, we only had thirty-eight seats and we could not crack the numbers we needed to. No matter how busy we were, we only had thirty-eight seats. We were trying to do French three-star in the middle of Key West, Florida, in 1988 and we were way beyond what people who were coming to Key West wanted [us] to be. We got great write-ups but the local people just did not get it. During this glory time of being Florida's first published chef, Mira had to close. This temporarily ruined us financially and I felt that I lost the town that I once lived in, and I lost the place that we worked so hard on and wanted to work in, and lost what seemed to be the future I wanted to have. You know I have to say I married a woman who has amazing strengths, and we eventually pulled out of that and persevered and opened up Norman's a few years later.

"The last few years have been the most rewarding time for me. In many ways [it is] because I have become much more comfortable and my work has become more understood. What I have tried to achieve, I have accomplished. More importantly being married to the same person for thirty-five years and [having] an incredible son who is in business with us . . . and I am able to spend much more time with them than I have over the years. There were times when I had to live in the same hotel where the restaurant was all week and only see the family on weekends, so this has been the best time."

If you listen closely to the words of Chef Norman, you can hear how difficult this was. When something does not work out, our first instinct can easily be to quit. That is the easy way out. This is one quality that fortunately none of the champions ever acquired. They never quit, they learned and moved on. They got over the bump—and sometimes mountains—and moved on. Let's listen to Chef Norman's final words and advice.

Leadership

Chef Norman had quite a bit to say on the topic of leadership. "I have had several employees who have come along and worked with me for about a year, [then] they would feel they have absorbed the lessons from the master and they're going to go out now [and] go for it. They would take all the recipes they could get their hands on and go. What happened at least three times is that they went out and got their teeth handed to them, and they came back and asked for their job back. This was an extraordinary lesson for them and those around them. Others would be quick to see that the once all-star executive sous chef had to come back with hat in hand. They would stay another two years and would then leave ready, a little more prepared.

"Some people look for success in results that are tangible. This is not the only place that results and success show up. They can be intangible, they can be relationships and friendships, they can be understandings. There is a lot to be said for the quiet lessons and victory too. I have been successful in ways that people could see and read about. I have had young people ask me, "Chef, how can I become famous?" Sometimes young people would see the effects of something, watch TV, or listen to the radio, or see a magazine with famous people and wonder how they can make that happen and be famous. You can't be worried about that. You have to find a passion and follow it, and if it is real, and if people care about it—because people do have to care about it, or it will never work—then it will occur, but only if you are passionate about what you're doing and what you love to do. Those who are setting out to be famous are only setting themselves up for a very disappointing failure.

"Some of my protégés and past employees have nicknamed my restaurant 'Norman's University.' Meaning that there has been much success of employees that have worked hard, learned the craft, and moved on to be successful."

"I take the high road because I like the view."
—Chef Norman Van Aken

Chef Norman's closing thoughts: "I was brought up a certain way, and that was to create a sharing and empathic atmosphere and hope for the best. I use much more honey than vinegar when working with people. You will not find many or any people who would say that I am violent or a screamer; I take the high road because I like the view. I feel that I can lead better when I am among them, I can be that good coach when I am working with my people. Stroke them and smoke them. Let the employees know when they do great and support them when they need support, and also let them know when they screwed up. Tell them when they have made a mistake, but don't make it personal. I think that has been my management style for years. I speak to all of my people as chefs and I will ask them questions to see if their mind is open and engaged. If it's not, I think the employee will sometimes be surprised at what I remember their answers were."

Chapter 6

Your Culinary Investment

Contacts! Contacts! Contacts!

What is your "culinary investment," you ask? Consider this analogy:

Joey hopes to make a lot of money one day. He only has $100 now. He knows that he will not make a lot of money for a while but that if he puts his money to work for him, his $100 will eventually be worth much more. So Joey carefully invests his money, and over a five-year period the $100 turns into $1,000.

Now don't focus on the money in this analogy. The point is: This is why your plan for what happens directly after graduation is so important. If you do not carefully plan your first five years after graduation, you may find yourself not making much more money than when you first graduated. Your "culinary investment" is flat, it did not make much money for you, and you did not grow professionally. Lack of a plan + lack of focus = failure!

> Lack of a plan + lack of focus = failure!

It is not common and certainly not recommended for recent graduates to become sous chefs or executive chefs directly after graduation. Instead, consider the first five years after graduation as an investment toward your culinary success. I have seen too many new culinarians come through my kitchens without a long-term plan. Simply understanding the concept of a plan could be the one thing that will guarantee your success, when combined with your work ethic. I have been doing this for a while, even if it has been more than five years since I finished culinary school.

> Consider the first five years after graduation as an investment toward your culinary success.

So many times new professionals miss the boat. Too many times graduates think they have done everything necessary to succeed by simply going to school and getting good grades. Then they enter their field and wait for the skies to open up and reward them with excellence. Great for you if this ever happens, but more often the great job opportunities and contracts go to those who carefully plan their future and work their tail off until they get them.

Your culinary education did a great job preparing you with a wonderful basic knowledge of culinary fundamentals. But your instructors can only provide you with the tools; you still have to manually use them. They cannot go out and do the work for you—that part is up to you.

> Your instructors can only provide you with tools; you still have to manually use them.

Landing Your First Job

Landing your first job out of school can sometimes be nerve racking. It is a crucial time in your life. I have to admit my earlier career was blessed. I don't really know why, but it just was. The three jobs I have held in my career have been absolutely wonderful experiences and fantastic opportunities. But on the other side of that coin is a boatload of hard work, determination, and lots of "table chewing." My career has been blessed, but it came as a result of a lot of hard work.

> "The road to success is dotted with many tempting parking places."
>
> —Author unknown

As I mention throughout this book, there is no substitution for experience. So the only thing you can do is: Go after it! Go after the experience with full force, grab it, learn from it, and grow. The most important thing is not to waste your time being unfocused. Don't find yourself wandering aimlessly, punching in and punching out, with no goal or vision as to what you are doing.

Which job would you take directly after graduation?

Job A:

> An executive chef's job in a small property, supervising a staff of ten employees. The salary would start at $40,000. The job is pretty cut and dried. Not much experience needed, because all the menus are written by the corporation and are relatively simple. All you need to do is supervise ten employees, maintain food and labor costs, and be sure to order the food that is specified by the company. The job description would not change over the years because it is a chain property, and they all use pretty much the same menus and concepts.

Job B:

> Entry-level line-cook job at a well-respected, privately owned restaurant. Job pays ten dollars an hour. This restaurant is packed every night and has a one-month waiting list for reservations. The chef is nationally known and runs a very disciplined kitchen. All recipes are from scratch and the menus change daily. Sous chefs from this restaurant have moved on to open their own restaurants and have been incredibly successful.

> "Experience is not what happens to a man. It is what a man does to what happens to him."
>
> —Aldous Leonard Huxley

There are a lot of young culinarians who feel they need to go for the money. But from which experience do you think you would most benefit? Learning under a mentor directly after graduation would be the best choice if you want to learn how to cook. To me, it is obvious; is it obvious to you? That is not to say that working for a fine dining restaurant chef is the only way to go. You must make your decisions based on what would be the best opportunity for you to grow as a professional in the culinary arena you wish to pursue. If you want to become a manager or general manager of a fast food chain restaurant and eventually buy a franchise, then you need to do research and find the most successful operations out there. Find the companies that take great care of their employees and have management teams known for mentoring. The same formula goes for any avenue that you wish to pursue: resorts, hotels, freestanding restaurants, chains, clubs, and so on.

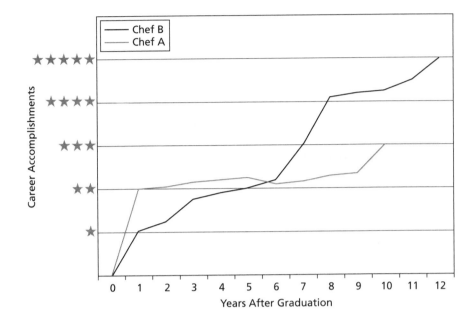

Take a look at the graph above. This is not a scientific graph by any means. It is just a picture of what I have seen over and over again in my years of mentoring young professionals.

FLAT LINE

Chef A in the chart indicates Joey, who decided to go for the $40,000 salary. Over the span of five years, Joey flat lines with compensation and overall knowledge of being a great chef, because the company he went to work for has no real growth potential. More importantly, Joey has a difficult time getting any other job offers; his experience is not necessarily the standard that prospective employers look for. Joey is having a hard time "climbing the ladder" because no one trusts his background. I call this "flat line."

Chef B indicates Josie. Josie decided to do the research and find the chef who best fit her dream. Josie found a very successful chef whose priority is food and who is well documented as a mentor for young culinarians. The pay was only ten dollars an hour, but Josie's plan was to win the confidence of the chef, who would then support her in her professional growth.

Josie had a two-year plan worked out with the restaurant chef. The plan was to work her tail off and learn every station in the restaurant. Her goal was to learn each station better than the person teaching her! (Sound familiar?) Josie came to work early and stayed late. She had to earn her stripes.

After two years, as agreed, the restaurant chef made a phone call to one of his very successful colleagues. He told this chef, "You have to hire Josie. She is unbelievable." And so goes another two years. Five years after graduation, Josie now has the confidence of two or three outstanding, well-respected chefs and all of the cooks in each establishment. On top of that, Josie has received culinary experiences that you cannot pay for.

Stealing Rolodexes

If I told you I know how you can obtain a thousand wonderful and talented names, addresses, phone numbers, and e-mail addresses of professional chefs all across the United States and the world, would you be interested? Of course you would. You want to know who the movers and shakers are in our business. You want to find out who the best people and the best properties to work for are, correct? You can do this by what I call "stealing Rolodexes."

Clearly you are not actually going to steal a famous chef's Rolodex. To "steal a Rolodex" is to create your own list of professional contacts. So how are you going to build your list of contacts? You do it with your work ethic.

> What, you may ask, is a Rolodex? I have learned over the years of speaking at many schools that I need to explain what Rolodexes are. Those who still can't let go of the outdated methods of storing names, addresses, and business cards use a card file mounted on a spindle, which is called a Rolodex, and it usually sits on top of their desk. The Rolodex typically holds the names of all their contacts, professional and personal. It is their version of "Contacts" in your phone or e-mail "address book."

THOUSANDS OF CONNECTIONS AND CONTACTS

Josie, from the previous story, has now proved herself at three outstanding properties over the past five or six years. She volunteered wherever she could. She went to work early and stayed late. Her work ethic was above and beyond all expectations, and uncompromising. She is simply an employee everyone can count on. Each of the successful chefs who hired Josie has a huge Rolodex on his or her desk totaling thousands of contacts. Everyone respects and has a deep admiration for Josie. Everyone who has worked with her is proud to be a part of her success. They are now willing to help Josie in any way possible because she has put in her time, she has proven herself.

Therefore, Josie now has all of the respect and many of the connections and contacts of all three chefs. Now that she is ready for her first executive chef job, imagine the help, the networking, the opportunities, and the references she will get.

What Is Your Reputation?

Greatness does not come in a forty-hour work week. Josie became successful because she gained the confidence and respect of all her mentors. She gained just as much of that respect out of the kitchen as she did while she was working in the kitchen. What does this mean? Josie spent those five years building and cultivating her reputation.

> "Don't be afraid to give your best to what seemingly are small jobs. Every time you conquer one it makes you that much stronger. If you do the little jobs well, the big ones will tend to take care of themselves."
>
> —Dale Carnegie

It is important that you understand that all the while you are working your way up the ladder, you are being observed by great chefs who can help you tremendously. All they know about you is what they see, your actions. Hopefully they will not only see you at work, but will also see you when you are volunteering, or at other functions outside of work. They will see how you carry yourself around your peers, how you act with other chefs and students, how you dress in and out of work. First impressions are golden, but second, third, and fourth impressions make an impact, as well. Furthermore, kitchens can be hives of gossip. What happens outside of the kitchen during your off-hours can find its way back into the kitchen.

Always remember, you are working hard to get ahead. You are putting a lot of time, money, and effort into climbing the ladder. That doesn't mean you can't have fun or blow off steam. But one wrong decision, being in the wrong place at the wrong time, could set you back and set back your five-year plan.

> Greatness does not come in a forty-hour work week.

I had a worker who I thought was a super kid. He was a hard worker, genuine, caring, and an all-around good person. He had a great work ethic. He was in his first year at the property and enjoying some great success. One night he found himself in the wrong place with some individuals who did not take their careers as seriously as he did. Long story short, one night he was in a car with the others when the driver of the car thought it would be fun to take a joyride on the golf course, which caused several thousand dollars' worth of damage. Around 2:00 A.M., the car was stuck on the golf course, and the worker was stuck in the car with the rest. This was not good. Although the worker was not the driver, his career at this property was over. A great opportunity wasted.

"Son, you've got a good engine, but your hands aren't on the steering wheel."

—Former Coach Bobby Bowden, Florida State

Another time, our property had just finished a successful weeklong event. It was a huge event feeding over thirty thousand people. The week could not have gone better. We had a sous chef who was a very hard worker and well on his way to success. He was not far from his first executive chef job. After this long week, the staff went out to celebrate the success at the local bar. The night went into the morning. The worker started to make his way out, but security would not let the valet give him his keys. Although security was actually doing him a favor, the worker, being a little stubborn, found a way around the system and eventually got his keys. Ten minutes later he was pulled over, handcuffed, and taken to jail for the night. He was later charged for DUI, and the next two years were painful, expensive, and trying for him. Meetings, court appearances, DUI classes, and challenges of getting to work without a car became his focus. He survived the ordeal and is back on track now, but that was two years of his life he wishes he had back.

"People are always blaming their circumstances for what they are. I don't believe in circumstances. The people who get on in this world are the people who get up and look for the circumstances they want, and, if they can't find them, make them."

—G. B. Shaw, *Mrs. Warren's Profession*, 1893

The bottom line is that you have to be careful. You have to work hard in and out of work. You are an adult. You are doing your best to be successful. Think about all of your choices in and out of work. This is your life. What is your reputation? What will your legacy be?

> What will your legacy be?

Your Game Plan

What's your game plan? Add the following items to the game plan you are creating for yourself.

- Continue to get advice from your instructors on what you should do after graduation. After school is finished, stay in touch with them. They have provided you with good advice and feedback while you were in school; they can and will continue to be good sounding boards once you've left school.
- Do you have all of the contacts from the chefs you have worked with? Your goal is to have access to all your chefs' Rolodexes and all of the connections in them.
- Obtaining the perfect job will take working a little harder, a little longer, continuing to research properties, working extra hours in the kitchen, and talking to chefs to find that perfect fit.

Chapter Lessons

- Consider the first five years after graduation as an investment toward your culinary success.
- Develop a work ethic that earns you the contacts of your mentors.
- Great job opportunities and contracts go to those who carefully plan their future and work their tail off until they get them.
- Go after opportunity rather than money.
- Greatness does not come in a forty-hour work week.

MRS. JOANNE HERRING

Against All Odds

This next champion has a very special story of
perseverance. In the must-see movie *Charlie Wilson's
War*, Joanne Herring is played by Julia Roberts, and
Tom Hanks plays Charlie Wilson. Many of the best
movies are based on true stories, and this one is
no different.

Joanne Herring

This is not fair to Joanne, but I am going to try to paraphrase her legacy.
In the late 1970s and early 1980s, Joanne's mission was to help Afghanistan
fight the Soviet Union, just a small goal for a Sunday afternoon. Can you
imagine where you would start, as a civilian, to fight any war, not to mention
one in Afghanistan? And guess what—she was successful! A wonderful,
sweet, beautiful, Southern belle from Houston not only made a difference
in the Soviet-Afghan War, but the Afghans were successful in their efforts
to protect their country. So your next question might be: How did she get
involved in such a Herculean effort? This is what she told me.

"My husband was the founder of Houston Natural Gas Company
that assembled pipelines. At the time, he was very interested in gas and
alternative fuels. We started going to the Middle East to make deals with the
Arab nations to investigate various kinds of ways to transport energy that
were less expensive. We met the heads of state of every country: Jordan,
Morocco, Pakistan, Afghanistan, Saudi Arabia, Kuwait, and the Emirates.
The [countries] I mentioned first didn't have any oil and the ones that did
have the oil were the Emirates, Kuwait, and Saudi Arabia. We met some of
the most important people in the world. My husband [was asked] if he would
serve as the consulate general of Pakistan and he laughed and he said that
he would be delighted to, but he had companies in twenty-six countries
and really didn't have the time. He recommended that they ask me. Well,
of course, this was [a Muslim] country and the last thing on this Earth they
would like to have as a consulate general would be a woman, me!

"But they didn't want to offend him, because they hoped he would drill in
their country. They said okay, we will take her. I got very interested; I decided
that if you take a job then you must do the job, and it all started from there."

Without getting into all of the politics, I asked Joanne how she managed to survive the layers of government and accomplish her goal. Certainly getting anyone to listen to her must have been a challenge.

"I decided if I was going to take the job, that I was going to make a difference. So I studied on what I could do for these people. What do I have to offer them? Well, I have contacts and I must do something for the very poor, because that's where the problem lies, usually. I asked myself, why is Russia interested in Afghanistan? There is nothing there and the president was very afraid of being invaded by the Russians. And there is not that much in Pakistan either. What did they really want? And at this point I looked at a map and I thought of the Strait of Hormuz, which is where most of the energy of the world passed through. And I realized if two ships sank in the Strait of Hormuz then energy to the United States would be cut off. If that happened then it wouldn't be just the air conditioners in our cars that would be affected. In fact, it could bring down our country, and our military would not be able to function either.

"When I went back to Washington [I] started talking about [how] this was the objective of the communists, not Afghanistan, not Pakistan, but the ability to fly from Pakistan to bomb the Strait of Hormuz. That's when they began to listen to me. It took me four years but what happened was that every time I would be turned away, every time somebody would laugh at me, and they did often, it made me want to work harder. And as a woman, who was I to be going to the head of the CIA, to the secretary of state and to the vice president of the United States? I was lucky enough to get an appointment then, which was the hardest thing on earth to do. Between an ordinary person and a congressman, or a senator or a secretary of defense or commerce, there was an army of aides and it was their job to protect their boss, and to get to them is the hardest job imaginable.

"But if you keep at it and you do your homework—if I had not made sense in my message to them and I could not point it out concisely and intelligently, through practice, I would have been turned out of their office in five minutes, they wouldn't listen to me. But because I did keep at it and kept talking to everybody, we finally broke through and started to get some help."

By now you know I am a fan of Joanne Herring. It just blows me away to know she was traveling the world meeting with presidents of countries. Imagine what it must have taken to fight, to plead her case, to study, to learn government protocol, to never be discouraged when a door slammed in her face, but instead to let it give her more strength. Joanne continues to fight for Afghanistan today.

"I am involved right now to rebuild Afghanistan so that the Afghans can become stronger again to protect their own country. My war this time has no guns. We are trying to produce for them food, water, education, medical care; and if they have that then the Afghans can fight for their own country against the terrorists. So, I am now fighting the battle again and again and I have been doing it for two years and have seen every door slammed in my face, and each time I have learned.

"The one thing I learned over and over in my life is that if you work longer and harder than anybody else you'll win, but you have to be able to let people laugh at you and you have to let them slam doors in your face, you have to let them embarrass you. You simply say, 'Well, I didn't make it that time but I'll make it next time,' and you will."

"The one thing I learned over and over in my life is that if you work longer and harder than anybody else you'll win."

—Mrs. Joanne Herring

"If you keep just slugging it out, no matter how many disappointments you have, you will win."

I was told by a chef, many years ago, that you have to pretend to be something before you can actually become it. You have to practice to be successful and work hard to be successful before you will achieve success. You can't just jump out of a box and accomplish your dream or be suddenly promoted into the ultimate job, not if you haven't been thinking about it, and pretending to be that person. I have lived by these thoughts, and Joanne has her version of what has helped her.

Joanne's advice is to "Envision problems. Envision success. This is something I learned from the great Jim Thorpe, who was the first Native American to win in the Olympics. He said that he always saw himself winning, imagined himself running hard, saw himself making all the proper moves before he actually accomplished them. He saw himself crossing the finish line first before he even ran the race. He first learned how to do it, prepared himself to be as good as he could be, then he saw himself actually doing it in his mind. This was his secret to his success and I believe in this practice. Decide what you are going to do and go through it in your mind."

"Decide what you are going to do and go through it in your mind and envision your success."

—Mrs. Joanne Herring

Over the years I have set a lot of goals for myself, each one leading to the next. Each time I reach a level of success, for a moment I stop and say, "Wow this is great, I did it." But then I realize I am not done. Don't ever catch yourself being satisfied with "right now." Be encouraged by your success but never stop; you can always accomplish more. It can be a trap to be satisfied with what, at the moment, seems great. If you continue your quest, you realize that what you accomplished was pretty good, but that you quickly become much better if you just keep at it. I love what Joanne says about this idea.

"What happens is that you reach plateaus, you work, work, work and think 'I am going to make this, I am doing pretty well,' but then you hit a plateau. You think, 'Well, I can't get beyond this point, what's wrong with me?' But you just keep working and studying and preparing and then one day, [it's] just like opening a door, and then the next door will open and you pass through it. Every door opens, bam, bam, bam. You can't believe that suddenly, everything you have worked so hard for has happened. But the thing is that you were prepared, you worked longer and harder than [every]body. You had something to give and there is nothing free in this world. Anybody who thinks they are going to get something easy is wrong."

I hope you have enjoyed meeting Joanne Herring. Go see the movie, if you have not seen it. It is difficult to write only three pages on her. It is like trying to fill the Grand Canyon with sand using a teaspoon. Her stories are incredible but very real.

Chapter 7

Completing Your Degree

No Slacking!

Now that your externship is over, it is time to buckle back down to your last stretch of school. School should become more exciting with some hands-on experience under your belt.

Reuniting with your friends and exchanging experiences will be great as well. Learn about your friends' experiences and find out how their externships went. Find out all the positives and negatives they experienced. Learn about the kitchen environment and the leadership styles of the chefs they worked with. You never know, you may be interested in one of those properties for future employment. The more information you get, the better off you will be.

Now is the perfect time to reassemble the "Leadership Team" to compare notes on the externships. Look at all the research you have been doing up to this point. You have compiled information on great chefs and different avenues of employment. You have studied different properties for potential employment. You have organized sit downs with all your instructors, and you have developed binders on Building Your Resources. Now is the time to start your research on the different properties where your Leadership Team has worked and the experiences they've had. This is all part of developing your own Library of Excellence. Just think how far ahead of your peers you will be as you continue adding to and building this library. Your basic knowledge will be light years ahead of everyone else's if you follow through. The key point here is that you have to follow through.

> Your basic knowledge will be light years ahead of everyone else's if you follow through.

Discipline

I can spot right away the difference between the young chef who has done all the work and the one who didn't. I can determine within the first few minutes of an interview which candidate has done the research on my property, who has the drive and eagerness to learn, and who takes advantage of all the opportunities presented in the school and kitchen environments. Most importantly, I can sense who has developed a personal discipline that will set this one culinarian apart from all the rest. This discipline is what will shine through someone's work and make him or her a great employee. It will work toward making that person a great leader to other chefs.

> Develop a personal discipline that will set you apart from all the rest.

NO SLACKING!

School may be almost over, but that doesn't mean you can slack off. You can have fun and enjoy yourself, but don't skip the exercises you started at the beginning of your culinary education. Keep everything in perspective. Don't let your grades or focus fail because of it.

CLASS BONDING

It is a powerful feeling to experience team building. Your classmates are part of your success, and they will be future contacts and resources for you. As you near the end of your formal education, you likely may experience a bond with the entire class. And if you do, it is a pretty cool feeling. I hope that you experience this because it is truly a special feeling. Don't graduate with any grudges. Don't graduate with bad memories. Find a way to pull everyone through successfully. Help those who need help. Pick those up who need a hand. Finish strong and finish happy; you will be glad that you did.

When my daughter received her National Honor Society credentials, she received a very cool t-shirt with the NHS emblem on the front and a very inspirational quote on the back. I want to share that inspiration with you:

> "To laugh often and much; To win the respect of intelligent people and the affection of children; To earn the appreciation of honest critics and endure the betrayal of false friends; To appreciate beauty, to find the best in others; To leave the world a bit better, whether by a healthy child, a garden patch, or a redeemed social condition; To know even one life has breathed easier because you have lived. This is to have succeeded."
>
> —Ralph Waldo Emerson

No Regrets

Don't graduate and regret that you failed to do better at any stage of your schooling. It is a terrible feeling.

At the same time, it is important to ask yourself if you got all the education you deserve, or at least took advantage of the various opportunities provided. Do you feel comfortable with all the basics you have obtained? Did you take full advantage of the school's library? Do you feel you need to have another sit down with an instructor who has been a tremendous mentor to you during school? Now is the time. Do not graduate and regret.

> "What this power is I cannot say; all I know is that it exists and it becomes available only when a man is in that state of mind in which he knows exactly what he wants and is fully determined not to quit until he finds it."
>
> —Alexander Graham Bell

Five years after my graduation, I returned to my alma mater to do some hiring at their job fair. As I was walking out of the library, I saw a former classmate running in with a stack of videos and books. After catching up, I asked him what he was doing with all of the videos. He replied, "Charles, back when we were going to school, I wasted half my time here. I never once stepped foot into this incredible library to take advantage of all of these videos and resources. Now I am just trying to get caught up a bit."

Don't graduate and regret, people. Go get it and stay focused! Keep chewing!

ADVICE FROM CULINARY EDUCATORS

Q: *What words of advice would you offer a graduate today when entering the culinary world for their first job?*

A: According to the 2008/09 U.S. Bureau of Labor Statistics, "Accommodation and food services is expected to grow by 11.4 percent and add 1.3 million new jobs through 2016. Job growth will be concentrated in food services and drinking places, reflecting increases in population, dual-income families, and the convenience of many new food establishments." This points to the existence of numerous jobs for culinary school graduates; however, alumnae must be selective about which jobs they take, as not all jobs advance careers. After identifying short- and long-term career goals, you must analyze your weaknesses and seek out opportunities that will round out your resume. Finding the best people in their fields, and convincing them to hire you is crucial for building a solid foundation. Don't gauge success in monetary terms; look at superior learning experiences as an equally important form of compensation. Make life interesting for yourself, now!

Robert Garlough

A:

- It is a privilege to work with food.
- It is the chef's kitchen, not yours.
- The customer IS always right.
- Don't ever sacrifice quality.
- Treat ingredients with respect.
- Treat your co-workers with respect.
- Learn something new every day.
- The foundations will never do you wrong.

Paul Sorgule, CEC, AAC

A: Give your boss what he or she needs to be successful. Be patient with your career choices. Most young employees are unprepared to be patient and trust that the road to success will be paved by their own performance. If on a daily basis they perform at a high level they can move fairly fast in the hospitality industry. Don't be too quick to think the grass is greener somewhere else, but always weigh your options when opportunity arises. Look to work for a large employer or property early in your career. Entry-level employees in large properties see more and can do more than with small employers. This is valuable early in a career as one can gain versatility!

Kirk T. Bachmann

A: All the normal must-do's like be on time, look the part, stay alert, always—and I mean always—look interested, and, of course, be interested. This is the beginning of you making a career for yourself [so] take it seriously.

William Gallagher

A: I know some young chefs who are quick to announce they only want to do "their food." These individuals often find themselves without a job. Never forget that feeding our guests and associates is our job. It is our individual service to others that helps create a foundation for understanding community and how we fit into it.

Work out, tune the machine you bring into work every day. You'll surpass expectations and find success,

Daniel Hugelier, CMC

Don't Ever Forget Where You Came From

Graduate with class. Be proud of your accomplishments; be grateful for your new friendships. But most of all, don't ever forget where you came from. Write thank-you notes to the instructors who had the most impact on your education and aspirations. Be sure to shake their hands and thank them. They are a very important piece of your education and foundation as a culinarian. Be grateful that they are passionate about what they do.

> Don't ever forget where you came from.

THE POWER OF THANK-YOU CARDS

If you go through life and don't acknowledge or care about those who have inspired you, helped you become successful, and guided you to where you are today, you will not go far. It is true that the more you give, the more you get. If you want to receive, you have to give. Along the path to success, you need to be grateful to those who have helped you. Besides, everyone who has helped you, you want as a friend forever. Please (please, please) take the time to write handwritten notes thanking them for their influence on you.

> "Promise me you'll never forget me because if I thought you would I'd never leave."
>
> —Winnie the Pooh

Yes, handwritten notes. Despite this digital age, a handwritten note makes a positive impact and impression on the person who receives it. E-mails are OK and acceptable, but there is a lot to be said for somebody who actually takes the time to sit down and write a personal note.

> The more you give, the more you get.

I have written to famous chefs, authors, Culinary Olympic chefs, TV personalities, professional athletes, and coaches to let them know how much they have inspired me one way or another. And they have written back. In many cases, I have developed, kept, and maintained personal relationships with these people, and we enjoy great relationships today. Don't ever underestimate how special a personal card is. It shows that the sender has a lot of character.

> Don't ever underestimate how special a personal card is.

Your Game Plan

What's your game plan? Add the following items to the game plan you are creating for yourself.

- Make a promise to yourself that you will finish your education strong. Be sure you take the last few months just as seriously as the beginning months.

- Make a personal evaluation of what you have learned. Run through all the notes from the entire years of school. Double-check that you thoroughly understand all the classes and be sure you're not graduating with any regrets.

- Write thank-you cards to those who have made an impact on your life while you have been at school.

Chapter Lessons

- Learn and study all of your colleagues' extern experiences.
- Continue to build your resources and your Library of Excellence.
- Develop a personal discipline that will set you apart from all the rest.
- Don's slack off near the end of school; finish strong.
- Bond with your classmates; develop great memories.
- Don't graduate with regret.
- Don't ever forget where you came from or who helped you succeed.
- Write thank-you cards to all instructors who made a difference in your life and also to your loved ones who supported you in school.

MONICA POPE
Chef and Owner of T'afia Restaurant, Houston, Texas

Meaningful Food

Monica Pope

One of America's most accomplished chefs is based in Houston. You can go online and read all about Monica Pope and all of her incredible accomplishments. She is a very special person who is not in the business for the stardom, although she is a star; she is not in it for the money, although she has done well running two restaurants continuously for eighteen years; she is not in it for the ego trip of having the best food in town, although she does have some of the best; she is simply in it because she deeply loves food. You can spend hours listening to Monica talk and learning from her passion.

I asked her how she first got interested in food.

"I was a swimmer and I swam until my sophomore year of high school and had a pretty rigorous workout schedule. I felt the separation between me and my family because of the commitment to swimming. I would work out at 5:00 o'clock in the morning and then again at 6:00 o'clock at night, so when I got home around 9:00 I would have to microwave my dinner. After a while I figured out that this isn't what I wanted to pursue in college.

"So when I stopped swimming I found myself getting more involved with my family and started cooking for them. My junior and senior year I went to visit my grandmother, who was Czechoslovakian, and she did a lot of traditional food. I wanted to learn from her; something in me wanted to preserve her traditional style of food.

"My initial interest was to bring the family back to the dinner table and carry on some family traditions that I thought were slipping away and very important to the family. I used to read a lot of cookbooks and felt like cooking, for me, was a calling, if you will."

Seasonality, Celebration, and Hospitality

Sometimes I think all great champions think the same. Chef Paul Prudhomme talked about how passionate he was about food and how special it was to bring the family together at the table. The same is true with Monica. She seemed to have a calling very early in life.

"I remember my roommate in college asking me what I was going to do after graduation and I told her that I was going back to Houston and change how people eat. At the time I didn't know what that meant, it was like somebody else was saying it, but I knew that's what I wanted to do.

"So after graduation I traveled around the world for ten years, spending most of my time in Greece and London. Then I came back to Houston twenty years ago to open my first restaurant. I have had two restaurants for eighteen consecutive years."

It takes a pretty focused individual to make such a statement while still in college. To want to change the way people eat means knowing the history of food and having the insight as to where you think it should go. And that is what Monica did. I asked her about the biggest lesson during her culinary ventures.

"One of the biggest lessons and probably the most fortunate I learned [is] that it's not just about the food. You have to connect with people on many different levels. We decided many years ago that we were going to anchor ourselves to seasonality, celebration, and hospitality. I love to cook, I love good food and I love great wine.

"One of the most difficult things is that you have to push the food out, you have to get it out, even on your worst day you have to produce. It's an unforgiving business in that respect.

"That's how I have been trained my whole life, that you put your head down and swim to the other side of the pool and get there as fast as you can.

"I feel like I have a responsibility, especially during these tough economic times, not only to my restaurant but to my people. That's one of the biggest lessons to remember, that we are here because there are people that want us to be here. We have to remember that the person coming through that door, you have to really take care of."

"That's how I have been trained my whole life, that you put your head down and swim to the other side of the pool and get there as fast as you can."

—Chef Monica Pope

"I think I attract employees who like to work and want to work. Mostly, I believe it's because I am right there with them working every day. I work hard every day and my employees see that and I think respect me for it, and I respect them. The people who come to work at my restaurant really want to work."

I love the fact that Chef Monica realized very early on that they needed to develop the restaurant standards and beliefs as a team. This core value speaks for itself.

I asked Chef Monica what message she had for young culinarians.

"Just do good work. There is good food and then there is great food and then there is meaningful food. Ask yourself, 'Who are you, what are you, and what are you really about?' I would like more people doing really good work, more thoughtful food and what is really meaningful to them."

> *"Just do good work. There is good food and then there is great food and then there is meaningful food. Ask yourself, 'Who are you, what are you, and what are you really about?'"*
> —Chef Monica Pope

"Just because you worked for someone great like a celebrity chef doesn't mean that you deserve success. Who are you, really? For me, I have worked with many chefs and I have tried to take from them and their experience to help form who I really am.

"Have fun, be creative. I would really like to see the young people of today be connected to their food and where it comes from. Try to find a way to express who they are."

Chapter 8

The Real World

Comfortably Persistent

Congratulations!!! You did it! You have graduated with great recommendations from your instructors and from your externship. You have completed the first step in your culinary career. Now it is time for the real world, where acting like a student no longer is allowed. You will always be a student of the craft, but your responsibilities have now changed. You are now on the way up the industrial ladder.

> You will always be a student of the craft, but your responsibilities have now changed.

The Interview

Before you can attack your first job, you have to be offered a job. I want to talk about the interview process. You probably will go through many interviews over the coming years. Some people interview better than others. Some people love to interview and I am one of them. Some people freeze up and don't represent themselves well at all. You need to be ready for your interview in order to make a great impression. Let's talk about some ideas that will help you succeed.

> You need to be ready for your interview in order to make a great impression.

Your resume needs to be clean and professional. It needs to include your externship and list what references you have collected so far. Make sure there are absolutely no spelling errors. Don't fill the resume with fluff. Chefs will read right through it. Don't pretend you have more experience than you really have. To be honest, I hire on the heart and rarely on the resume. I will take a cook with little experience but a big heart, one who will give me 100 percent all of the time. I will take a cook with less experience any day over the hotshot superstar who is looking to come in and teach me something and change my systems.

> I hire on the heart and rarely on the resume.

Don't get me wrong; I learn every day. I learn from my people every day. I encourage my people to participate and help make changes in our kitchens. But I am not looking for someone who is only interested in showing his or her arrogance and does not respect the staff. I will not tolerate it. I do, however, embrace an employee's eagerness to excel, to be great. There is a difference.

> "We receive three educations, one from our parents, one from our schoolmasters, and one from the world. The third contradicts all that the first two teach us."
> —Charles Louis de Secondat, Baron de Montesquieu

When going for your interview, you know by now that you go in prepared. Be on time. Know the route and be aware of how much time it takes to get there. You want to get there early, but don't show up in the chef's office until the scheduled time. There is a good chance the chef has a pretty tight schedule, so if you come forty-five minutes early, it will not be convenient in most cases. Get to the property early, but show up exactly on time for the interview.

You have the complete background of the chef. You know where he started, what properties he has worked at, where he got his education, and, possibly, who his mentor was. You are aware of what awards she has won and what her menus are like. You want to be able to reference some of these facts during the interview. Chefs love to hear that you have done your research; they love to hear about themselves. If you are able to go into the interview and reference an article the chef was in or an award she recently received, or if you can recite parts of her menu, you will get the chef's attention.

> "Success seems to be largely a matter of hanging on after others have let go."
>
> —William Feather

Do not over-talk. Talk for the sake of talking will bury you. The chef will ask you questions, and those are probably the questions he or she wants the answers to. Speak when spoken to. Try to answer directly. Do not fluff all around the question with a bunch of mumbo jumbo that has nothing to do with the subject. Be honest. Be genuine about the fact that you are there interviewing strictly because of the chef. You are there because you want to take the next step in your career and want to be mentored by this person. At some point the chef will ask you if you have any questions. Bring a list with you of points that you have been thinking about. It is OK to pull it out; it will show that you were prepared.

Let the chef see the personal side of you. Try not to be nervous. Enjoy the process. Be passionate about who you are. Take notice of the office surroundings. At some point you may want to make reference to a particular award or photograph you see there.

> Be passionate about who you are.

MONEY

Do not talk about it! One rule, during the first interview: Please don't talk about money. If the chef wants to talk about money, he or she will bring it up. If not, that may mean the chef is not sure about the interview or feels that you may not be the right fit. If this is the case, your focus should be on winning the interview, not on what the pay is. It is a complete turn-off to a chef who has just spent an hour with a prospective employee—touring the property and kitchens, talking about the philosophies of the property, kitchen, and food—when, upon asking if there are any questions, the first thing he or she hears out of the prospective employee's mouth is: "How much?" This instantly tells the chef that this person is not interested in learning or growing at the property, only in making money.

> "Difficult things take a long time, impossible things a little longer."
>
> —Author unknown

DRESS FOR SUCCESS

Be well groomed. Men, be clean shaven and wear a suit if you have one; women, wear a pantsuit or dress. Do not come in jeans or have the four-day beard working. It's not cool. Depending on the property, there may be a policy against visual body piercing, so keep it simple. I am going to drive this point home because it is important. A handwritten thank-you card or note is a standard procedure that has gone by the wayside. It does take time and a little effort, but it makes a huge, positive impression. I recently wrote some cards to some instructors who were nominated for a very special award. I saw one of them later in the year. He was quite impressed that I took the time out of my schedule to recognize him. He was so touched by it that he brought the card in the next day to class and spent the whole class on how important it is to handwrite cards.

COMFORTABLY PERSISTENT

If you, at first, are denied a position, be comfortably persistent. If you are a recent graduate and you know this is the job for you—you have done all the research, and you want this job more than anything—go after it. It can be as simple as contacting the chef once a week or once a month to let him or her know you are still interested in working at the facility.

> If you, at first, are denied the position, be comfortably persistent.

I have had students who knocked on my door every week until I finally gave them a shot. They would say things like, "Just give me a shot, Chef, I will prove to you I can do the job. I will work anywhere. Can I stage (work for free) so you can see how hard I work?" After these students kept calling once a week for about a month, I hired them when I had a vacancy.

> "I have been up against tough competition all my life. I wouldn't know how to get along without it."
>
> —Walt Disney

They wanted it more than anybody else, and proved it to me. But there is a fine line between proving your passion and being a pain in the behind. Just don't cross that line. You have to be careful in this respect. You don't want to anger and annoy the chef, but you do want to prove to him or her that you want the job more than anything. A call once in a while, a follow-up e-mail, and an occasional card always help. Just always remember to be polite and comfortably persistent.

Your Game Plan

What's your game plan? Add the following items to the game plan you are creating for yourself.

- Now the only thing you need to worry about is your game plan. THE PLAN! If your plan is solid, if you have an idea of where you want to work and for whom you want to work, if you've acquired all the contacts you can along the way, then you're going to be in great shape. Now it's time to put all of this into practice.

- Up to this point, you have done a lot of research about the chefs you admire and the area of the industry in which you are most interested in working. Now that you are starting to interview, it's vitally important to do plenty of research about the specific property and chef you are trying to get a job with. Be professional: Know as much as there is to know about the property where you are interviewing and the chef who runs the kitchen. Show that you care and be prepared.

- A few months after getting your first job, when you have had a chance to show your incredible work ethic, schedule a sit down with your boss and share your plan, to enlist his or her support toward helping you be successful.

Chapter Lessons

- You need to be prepared for your interview in order to be successful.
- Know the complete background of the chef.
- Do not over-talk.
- Be genuine.
- Have a prepared list of questions.
- Do not talk money.
- Be on time.
- Write a thank-you note.
- Be comfortably persistent.

CHARLIE FRAZIER

Pro Bowl Wide Receiver, Houston Oilers

Any Given Sunday

Charlie "The Razor" Frazier

I was driving to a Houston Texans home football game one Sunday with my daughter, and we heard the most amazing story on the radio. It was an interview with a Pro Bowl wide receiver who played for the Houston Oilers from 1962 to 1968. The interviewer asked Charlie Frazier what college he had played football for, and the answer blew me away. I had a chance to talk to him, and he told the story again.

"I was in school and two of my friends were football players, but I didn't play football in college. I ran track. We were going to summer school at the time. The Oilers were getting ready for training camp and my two friends wanted the opportunity to try out, so they were walk-ons. I went because I thought it would be exciting to watch them. I was sitting in the stands when Mr. John Green walked by and asked me if I played ball, and I told him, 'No, I don't.' He asked, 'What do you do, then?' I told him that I was a sprinter and ran track. He then asked me what some of my times are and I told him. He said, 'Get out there and catch a few balls.' I said, 'Yes, sir!' and the rest is history. I was in summer school as a senior trying to finish up my degree, and the very next season I was playing pro football.

"I did play high school football, and almost got a scholarship but I was also offered the scholarship for track and I took that one, but in fact I was not allowed to play football in college, if you will, they said I could only run track."

Now imagine this for a second. Playing in the National Football League and never having played college ball. Those who play college ball dream every minute of the day about the possibilities of playing professionally, and here is a guy who never played college ball and walked on. And to boot, Charlie Frazier was five feet nine inches and 160 pounds soaking wet. In case you're not a football fan, take it from me, there is probably not anyone in the NFL today who is under 190 pounds. I asked Charlie about his size and if he was ever scared playing with athletes twice his weight.

Against All Odds

"I never was scared playing guys two or three times my size. I always felt that my speed would get me out of trouble. We had a scrimmage one day and I caught a pass on a slant pattern and got hit instantly by a 250-pound linebacker from LSU. Got hit, bounced up, and ran back to the huddle. I think at that moment, I felt like I could play in this league.

"The real challenge was actually making the team, 'cause I didn't think I had a chance. But after I got hit by that linebacker and I jumped up, one of the coaches came over to me and said, 'If you would just work a little harder, you may just make this team.' I thought I was already working hard. After he said that I thought that I obviously had a chance to make the team, so at that point I really put all my effort into it. Having only played high school football, I had so much to learn. I tried to become a complete player and emulate the guys [who] were so great."

Courage and Perseverance

The courage to chase your dream is one thing. The courage to fight a war with men twice your size is another. There are a few lessons I would like to recognize here. First, you can't let anyone get in the way of your dream. Second, getting hit incredibly hard, knocked down, then jumping up and letting everyone know how tough you are—and that you are here to stay—shows heart. I always say: Sometimes you need to pretend to be something before you can actually become it. You have to work hard and believe you belong, before you are accepted. You have to prove to your colleagues that you're the real deal and that, no matter what, they can count on you. I don't care if you're playing professional football, college volleyball, or peewee basketball, or if you're an apprentice chef in the kitchen, you are what your work ethic is.

> *"I tried to become a complete player and emulate the guys [who] were so great."*
>
> —Charlie Frazier

To aspire to emulate those who were so great is an important ambition. Charlie quickly recognized he needed to get better, so he sought out and studied the best and molded himself after them. He learned how the "greats" were working out and what they were doing for training. Is this starting to ring a bell? Study the people you want to be like. Research the chefs that you want to be like, and study what they did to be successful.

Focus on Greatness

Charlie went on to tell me, "There were some guys in the league [whom] I tried to emulate. Lance Alworth (a Hall of Fame player) from the San Diego Chargers was a great receiver and we had Ernie Ladd [who] came from the Chargers. Ernie used to tell me all the things that Lance did, and I couldn't wait to get on the field to try out those concepts. I had some guys I could look up to [whom] I wanted to be like, and I knew they were great and I wanted to be just like them."

Again this formula for success continues to creep into all the champion stories I share with you. If you can figure out the formula, you can make the recipe, correct? Well, this formula is more than just words. Everyone has heard what it takes to be successful and to be a champion, but oftentimes we just hear the words; we don't absorb them and live by them. This is what makes the difference between average and extraordinary. It would make me sad to me to know you had a dream but chose not to pursue it. Although the real sadness may come when we find out why you did not chase the dream. Was it because of fear, lack of focus, or just plain laziness?

What Is Your Uniqueness?

Charlie found what he was really good at, and that was speed. Charlie found his "uniqueness," which is what made him special, what separated him from others. So find out what makes you unique and market it, go after it. Charlie was so fast, his speed was so lightning-fast, that it won him a spot on the Pro Bowl team in 1966. But his speed was still something he had to work at. He had to develop it. He knew if he was going to have a chance to play in the NFL he had to work harder than anybody else because of his size and the lack of experience playing college ball.

"Most of my challenges had to do with athletics, mostly because I wasn't very good. I lived out in the country and what we did for fun on Friday afternoons was to run around the block. That was our entertainment. And I am ashamed to say, I couldn't outrun a girl. But I kept working at it, and kept working at it until one Friday I was outrunning everybody. Then another boy came along. He was a senior and I was a junior and we would race the hundred-yard dash. It appeared that he couldn't beat me, and I couldn't beat him. And it got so crazy that every Friday, kids would start to line up to watch us race. That was motivational and very challenging.

"I worked hard in my life and after I made the team I wanted to be sure I stayed on the team. In the off-season, though, I also worked for the school system because I didn't know how long I was going to be here . . . and always thought I needed something to fall back on just in case this didn't work out. So, I went ahead and applied in the school district. I played football in the fall and taught school in the spring. After work I would go over to the track and just run and run and run. I wanted to be sure that when training camp got started I was in the best shape possible. Speed was my weapon so I had to be sure I was the best I could be."

This brings up a tremendous point, and that is: Don't ever take anything for granted. Charlie was given a fantastic opportunity and he was not about to waste it. He was determined to work harder than anybody else, even during the off-season. He was going to go against all odds of size by continuing to train himself to be the fastest he possibly could be. But even the best of work habits sometimes aren't enough.

The "Stickability" Thing

Charlie went on to tell me, "I think one of the basic lessons is that once you start something you want to try to see it through, regardless of how tough it may be. You got to keep on plugging, you got to keep on trying. The reason why I say that is that in 1964, I got cut from the team. They put me on what they call the 'Taxi-squad' and I was on it for four or five games. But I continued to do the things I thought were a must during practice, worked hard and, as much as I could, stayed after practice with the quarterbacks. And then some of the guys started to come up to me to say, keep doing what you are doing and sooner or later something would break. So, this is what I did, and I had encouragement from some of the other players.

"That's the stick to it part, because once you start something you should see it through.

"In 1966, I ended up making the Pro Bowl, third in the league in receptions, second in the league in touchdowns."

Stick to it! Stickability. Do you see why I get so excited about this? I will say again and again that the difference between the average person and a champion is "Stickability"! Work hard, work hard, and work harder! If you want to be great, work hard and you will be who you want to be. Can you imagine? Charlie got cut from the team, and two years later made the Pro Bowl team. Simply amazing.

"That's the stick to it part, because once you start something you should see it through."

—Charlie Frazier

One more point, Charlie says, is if you start something, see it through! Finish it. If you start, finish no matter what. Drill that into the core of your being. Make that statement part of your core values and you will be successful.

Charlie's advice for students:

"First, I would tell them to stay in school. And second, if they work hard, enough things will eventually start to change for them. If you don't know the answer to something, go ask, and confide in someone, and I think that things will work out. My family has always given me a tremendous amount of support. My principal and my coach, they instilled in me a lot of the qualities, be strong and do what you are supposed to do."

Chapter 9

Achieving Success

Don't Cry over Spilt Milk

We have all experienced great movies in which individuals overcame all odds and hardships to become *great*. Remember the movies you have seen where the star actor or actress went from rags to riches or from a broken home in the slums to a massive mansion in a luxurious neighborhood? What is one common thing in these movies? There is always fantastic sound that you can almost feel, and there is always great music that just takes your breath away in a way that makes you dream. The music is so powerful that it sometimes brings tears to your eyes as you are watching the story unfold and the once "against-all-odds" character rises to the top and becomes successful. The character who never seemed to have a chance has achieved the impossible.

And then we wake up. The lights come on and we walk out of the theater. The powerful sound is gone and there is no music playing as we set foot back into the real world.

We all want to achieve success. But how do we know when we are successful? What are the clues? There is no music that will pick you up and make you successful in real life. There is no music or powerful sound that will be waiting for you at the end of your day that will signal your success. It is just you making the difference. You have to play the music yourself. You have to write the script and plan the ending yourself. It is up to you to make an impact on your own life and not wait for someone to do it for you. Good things happen to good people and to people who work hard.

> You have to write the script and plan the ending yourself.

Inspiration

Sometimes we are not searching for inspiration, but inspiration finds us. I want to share one of my experiences with you.

Sometimes we are not searching for inspiration, but inspiration finds us.

When I was in high school, I took a culinary arts course in which my father was the chef instructor. One thing my father did every year in his class was show a Culinary Olympic movie. I was a junior in high school and I knew instantly that I wanted to become a competition chef. When I saw those chefs cooking against the clock, competing against great chefs from all over the world, I knew I wanted to be one of them. I had no idea how or when, I just knew I wanted to do it.

Each year my father took a few students who wanted to compete to a food show in Boston, Massachusetts. At the time, the Boston show was the biggest food show in the country. My senior year I competed in a professional category.

That morning after I set up my culinary display, I walked around to see some of the booths being set up. I saw a chef behind one of the tables wearing a chef jacket with a red, white, and blue collar, and around his neck was a Culinary Olympic gold medal. I quickly ran over to introduce myself to the chef. His name was Chef Clark Bernier. I asked him if it, indeed, was a Culinary Olympic gold medal, and he acknowledged that it was. I asked him if I could hold it, and he took the medal off his neck and passed it to me. I was in awe. I said to him, "Chef, one day I am going to get me one of these gold medals."

Chef Bernier smiled and said to me, "That's great; if you believe and work hard, you can do it. Don't give up until you get it." He handed me his business card and told me to call anytime if I ever needed any help reaching my goals. I was smiling ear to ear.

I remember, as if it was yesterday, being so excited to have met a Culinary Olympic chef and to have held his gold medal. It was awesome.

Later that day I found out I had placed second and won a bronze medal in my category. I was on cloud nine. I was elated by my accomplishment as a student in a professional category. That was it; I had competition in my blood.

I saw the prestigious judges walking around in their lab coats, critiquing the contestants. I waited patiently to hear what I could do to improve. When the judges came over, they were not expecting to see a student. They were very generous and supportive of my accomplishments. They gave me encouragement to continue. Then something weird happened.

As the judges started to walk off, I told the judge closest to me about my dreams and goals. I told him that I wanted to go to the World Culinary Olympics in Germany and win a gold medal.

The chef stopped and turned back to me and said, "This table is a far cry from the World Culinary Olympics. Keep your goals tangible and worry about the basics and you will do fine. The Olympics are a far cry from this show." He patted me on my shoulder and gave me that "atta boy" tap and moved on.

He could have jumped off a ten-foot ledge and landed on my stomach—it would have felt the same. I was mad, disappointed, and deflated. I remember so vividly how disheartened I was. I went from the highest high to a deflated low. As I started to break down my table, I decided to ask the Olympic chef for some words of encouragement. I saw Chef Bernier reaching down to pick up his briefcase, about to walk out. I stopped him and told him of my experience with the judge.

"Which judge was it?" Chef Bernier asked. I told him and he smiled.

"Don't worry, he doesn't have an Olympic medal either. He doesn't know what he is talking about." The chef had a grin on his face, and he made me smile too. It was his next few words I will never forget.

"Don't ever let the words of others dictate your future or limit your success. You'll do fine; just remember what I told you."

> "Don't ever let the words of others dictate your future or limit your success."
>
> —Chef Clark Bernier

And remember I did. I have kept his words to this day, several World Culinary Olympic gold medals and seven U.S. Culinary Olympic Teams later.

My point is, sometimes we get inspiration when we are not looking for it. The judge gave me inspiration that day. He gave me inspiration to go out and prove him wrong. To me that is the best inspiration, when someone tells me that it is impossible, or that my dream or goal is too far from reality. That is the best energy I can get.

I returned from my first Culinary Olympics—the youngest chef on the team at the age of twenty-four—with one gold medal and the New England Culinary Olympic Team finished number one in the world. Upon my return, I decided to sit down and write a note to the judge who once told me that my display was a far cry from the World Culinary Olympics. It went something like this:

Dear Chef,
I wanted to share with you my most recent success. I just got back from Germany, from the World Culinary Olympics, and our regional team was best in the world with 18 gold medals. And guess what, chef. I got one of them! I just wanted to thank you for our talk and critique in Boston. You inspired me that day, five years ago.
Thank you,

Charles M. Carroll

In the card I placed a picture of me with the gold medal around my neck. While it was tempting to be derogatory in the card or angry in tone, the truth of the matter was that he did inspire me that day. Good, bad, or indifferent, he inspired me, and I had him and Chef Bernier to thank for that.

> Success and greatness do not come in a forty-hour work week.

Winning my first Culinary Olympic gold medal was a wonderful success, but it came only after a lot of hard work and dedication. I would work sixty to eighty hours a week for my job and then work another twenty hours a week studying and practicing for the Olympic Team. I have been on that schedule for the past twenty-two years. Someone once said being on one Olympic Team gains you ten years' experience in a three-year time period. I will tell you that being on a team is an incredible feeling and opportunity that I would not trade for anything. The chance to represent the United States of America and work with incredibly talented professionals from all over the country was life-changing for me.

Whether you want to open your own restaurant, be on television, or be on a Culinary Olympic Team, whatever your dream is, you decide if you will be successful or not. You take the ball and run with it. You decide your own destiny. Maybe you will fail along the way, but you decide if you're going to get back up and run, or quit. Heck, it is easy to give up! It's much easier not to do something than to work hard to achieve it. It's much easier to put your energy into conceptualizing all the reasons you can't do something than to come up with the plan and energy to figure out how you can achieve it. To be lazy is easy and there are a lot of lazy people in the world. To achieve greatness takes more focus and heart. You decide.

> You decide your own destiny.

Choose to Be Positive

You are in control of how you think. That is an easy thing to say, but how many people actually control how their mind works? How many control almost any situation simply by exercising positive thinking? My wish for you is to approach your life and your culinary work with a sense of a new beginning. Start fresh now and think positive.

Approach your life and your culinary work with a sense of a new beginning.

Thinking positive, and the exercise of thinking positive, can work magic. In many cases, how you think will influence your destiny. So if you are constantly thinking negative thoughts or only expect the worst, chances are, what you think will come true. Thinking negatively also affects one's attitude. If you're thinking negatively, chances are you are a negative person and may have a bad attitude most of the time. And that bad attitude influences how those around you perceive you. Conversely, if you can find the silver lining in all situations, somehow something good will come out of what originally seemed terrible. If you're thinking positively, even when things don't go as planned, they will eventually work out. And never forget, there is much to learn from what does not work or go your way. People who think positive most of the time usually are pretty good-natured. And the magic is: If you think positive, more positive things will happen to you. If you continue to think negatively, more negative things will happen to you.

It's actually not that negative things magically appear if you are thinking negatively, rather that they are appearing and being amplified if you are constantly *looking* for negativity. Let me share a story to illustrate.

Every April we have an international tennis tournament at my club. It is a crazy week and we feed tens of thousands of people throughout the tournament. Last year we had the fortune of it ending on Easter Sunday. Joy, joy. We had five Easter Sunday brunches on top of the final day of the tournament! The week was incredible, all went fantastically smooth. The staff on Sunday was tired but fired up over the success of the week—high-fiving and hugs were everywhere. Someone brought in donuts and Starbucks coffee to share with the team. It was a great atmosphere.

LOOK FOR THE GOOD

At 10:30 A.M., one of my supervising chefs came into work. He went to a station he was in charge of, and the equipment he needed was not there. Within three minutes he managed to change the entire positive atmosphere into a negative one. Fingers were pointing, front-of-the-house managers and captains were involved, as well as my executive sous chef. What was shaping up to be a glorious day toward a successful week was gone.

I quickly dissolved the issue but was very upset. There is one lesson I learned a long time ago, and that is not to address a situation when you're angry, if you can help it. So the next day I had a meeting with the chef in my office. I told him that I was not happy with the way he handled the situation, and, before I could finish my sentence, he was defending his actions with great emotion. I quickly stopped him and told him I really was not interested in the why, how, or who of the problem. As a supervisor and one of my senior chefs, he needed to find a better way to solve challenges when they occurred. He then said something that made a light go off in my head. He said he prepares himself every day by waiting for the worst to happen, so that when it does, he will be ready for it.

Imagine going through life constantly waiting for the worst to happen, constantly searching for the worst, so you'll be prepared when it happens.

We all have a choice. We have a choice to look for what we want to look for. If you constantly look for the good in your life, what do you suppose you will find? If you constantly look for the bad in your life, what do you suppose you will find? Ultimately, life is your choice. What you choose to look for, you will find; what you find, you will attract; and what you attract, you will become! It is that powerful.

You have the choice to be positive; you have the choice to control your own life. If you constantly prepare yourself for the worst to happen, the sad thing is that you will miss many wonderful experiences in life because you fail to see them.

> So don't stop "looking"! Keep looking for the good, and you will find it.

One morning my daughter was pouring milk on her cereal, and she accidently dropped the container and milk went all over the counter. I quickly picked it up before the rest of the milk spilled. Where can you find the good in this story? It would be easy to get upset because everyone is short of time getting ready for work and school first thing in the morning. But I was thankful the milk did not go all over the floor! I was thankful the dog did not track it all over the house. It was a lot easier to clean up the counter than the whole floor, so I was thankful. I was thankful it did not spill all over our clothes. It could have been so much worse.

This is a simple example but a great exercise for you to think about. Constantly find ways to be thankful. If you train your mind to look for ways to be thankful, you'll find that you will be a much more positive person.

ADVICE FROM CULINARY EDUCATORS

Q: What do you think are the top challenges students face today in culinary and hospitality schools and in our workplaces, and what advice would you give to overcome them?

A: It has been estimated that there are 72,000 students currently enrolled in public and private culinary schools across the United States. Where this much interest exists, the presence of a national competition in both the classroom and the workplace also exists. Students who wish to excel in their careers must approach each day as a unique opportunity for learning, and they must not be complacent about their education or career. Successful students are driven to exceed, and thriving professionals have a sense of urgency. To rise above the rest, you must create a plan for success. Without your own plan, you become a tool in someone else's plan.

Robert Garlough

A: The first challenge is understanding the nature of the beast. It cannot be emphasized enough: this is a difficult business. Difficult physically, emotionally, and mentally. The glamour that is promoted on television is not the day-to-day reality. Yes, it is exciting and can be fun and gratifying, but they will work very, very hard throughout their career and MUST be prepared for that reality.

Understanding more about the product, history of cuisine, culture, etc. To know where the raw materials came from is to better understand how to work with them and appreciate them. To understand why certain methods are used because of culture or geography is to truly understand how to cook in an authentic manner.

Yes, it is all about the food, but it is also all about the business. Restaurants need to make money so all of those other courses like math, accounting, marketing, human resource management, and even psychology are as important as cooking foundations, classical cuisine, and menu design. Pay equal attention to these course contents.

Paul Sorgule

A: I would encourage students to select a school that offers a working restaurant, bar, dining room, coffee counter, simulated or actual hotel rooms, etc. I would also encourage students to look for a curriculum that includes robust focus on management, entrepreneurship, and cost control. Since most educational settings cannot provide all of these facilities, it is imperative that students work in at least one hospitality setting while attending college. Nothing will be as helpful to students' career paths as combining school and work experience as they head into the workforce. The fact that they are stable enough to manage work and school in addition to time spent in the industry will prove to be beneficial as they transition from student to employee to industry superstar!

Kirk Bachmann

A: Be familiar with the system within the USA and also in Europe. I would say the basic challenges for students entering both hospitality schools and, indeed, the workplace are very similar; those being understanding that the world today is very competitive in all aspects, especially performance. A young person is challenged to listen, absorb, and understand, not always having the opportunity to say those critical words, "**I do not understand—can you please explain that again to me?**" My best advice would always be if you do not completely understand, ask again until you get the answer you're comfortable that you understand.

Dr. William Gallagher, H.C.

PRACTICE SAYING THANK YOU

Let's say there is an employee constantly nagging you, asking a million questions you believe he should already have the answer to. This person seems to have a crisis almost every day. You have two options: You could be incredibly irritated with all the distractions, complain about the employee to your boss, dread every time this employee comes to you with his problems, and lose your temper with this employee. Or you can say, "Thank you."

You can practice saying thank you to yourself. "Thank you" that I have the patience to deal with this person. "Thank you" that I have a clear mind to answer his questions. "Thank you" that someone trusts me with his issues and has confidence that I can help him. "Thank you" that I have someone to teach and mentor.

You will be amazed how this makes you feel, if you use this tool every day, all day long. Say "thank you" when you wake up in the morning. Say "thank you" when you stand, for there are many people in the world who can't stand.

Train yourself to be thankful all the time. Even when times seem tough, find something to be thankful for. Say thank you that you have a great job, say thank you that your family is healthy. Say thank you as much as you can, all day long, and you will find you will be a happier person.

> "Chefs, as a whole, say yes to any project, fundraiser, or tasting because they have such a generous spirit."
>
> —Charlie Trotter

You will start feeling great, I promise. Be thankful now, insist on feeling good now. If something does not work well for you now, be thankful. You now know a way that does not work, and you can work toward a successful solution. If you feel yourself getting bogged down, starting to get negative, quickly find something to be thankful for. Imagine if your outlook on life was constantly finding ways to be successful and thankful. You will become what you think, and only you control what you think.

Don't ever catch yourself saying "I can't." If you say you can't, you won't for sure, so get it out of your head. Say "I can," and you will. If you don't succeed at first, you just became a little smarter. Keep saying "I can," and you will.

Remember, you choose whether you're going to be successful or not, nobody else. Nobody is going to tap you on the shoulder one day and say, "Congratulations, you're successful as of today." Only you can determine your success.

> You choose whether you're going to be successful or not, nobody else.

THE POWER OF GIVING

When you are just starting out in your career, your first instinct may not be worrying about those around you or their success. Your first instinct is to "survive." Be successful and survive. Do whatever it takes to work hard and get promoted, be thankful along the way and never forget where you came from. During this time frame it is understandable not to worry about the person next to you, not to coach, train, or mentor anybody because you are just trying to figure it all out yourself. However, you should pay attention to those around you. Learn from what others do, both right and wrong.

Once you have grown into a great chef, it is your duty to give back. I have seen individuals in the past whose sole purpose was to steal as much as possible and move on and up, not caring what or whom they step on along the way. This is really a terrible mentality and one that will eventually cause these individuals' downfall. If you want to be successful, you have to give. If you want to receive great things, you have to give great things.

> Once you have grown into a great chef, it is your duty to give back.

I remember one time I was hoping for a particular opportunity, and I shared my hopes with a special mentor of mine. I told him that I was not sure if I was going to get this opportunity but I was hopeful. He told me, "Give something away, help somebody soon, and it will come back to you." He made me smile and feel good about the opportunity. On the way home that night, I saw a homeless person sitting in a wheelchair at the corner stoplight. She had a pole with a basket at the end of it that she would extend out to the car windows. I stopped to give her some money, but the pole did not reach. Her shirt was torn and dirty. I got out of the car, reached into my back seat, and grabbed a sweatshirt out of my gym bag and gave it to her with some money. I now tend to do this sort of thing a lot. Two weeks later not only did I get the opportunity I was hoping for, but two others I was not expecting.

I also try to speak to students at culinary schools and colleges. This is what I love most. I know deep inside that I am making a difference in many lives. They come up and thank me and talk long after my presentation is complete. Many call and e-mail or write to me about their progress. This has been my mission over the past several years. This is what makes me jump out of bed in the morning. The idea of giving back and helping new culinarians is my passion. To mentor and be a part of someone's life, to share in their success, is something that nobody can ever take away from you. Help people, help your people, and start helping them today. Many people in your life helped you; now it is your turn. The more people you help, the more wonderful opportunities come your way. Read that last sentence again. The more you give of you, the more you get!

> The more you give of you, the more you get!

The power of giving. Find a way to give, but also be aware of those searching for help. Look for opportunities to give. I have found many ways to give back to my staff through the Green Beret Sous Chef Program and the Journeyman Program. These programs are a direct reflection of me and my work place., so it is important that these culinarians get as much of "me" as possible.

I have an opportunity to help other employees who are not doing so well. They may have ill family members, children with special needs, or problems they are struggling with themselves. I do my best when I can to give. These are all opportunities to help.

Recently I returned from working on a special fund-raising dinner for a very special nun named Sister Dulce. Sister Dulce is a remarkable person who touches, helps, and heals thousands of needy people around the world. We raised $240,000 in one evening. This will go a long way to help a lot of people. Not only was this the right thing to do, but I had the great opportunity to work with some fantastic people, such as Chef John Folse, who organized the whole event, as well as Chef Norman Van Aken, Joey DiSalvo, Hilmi Ahmad, and Rod Jesik. To break bread and cook with nationally known chefs is pretty special. It makes you want to give all the more.

> "Do what is right, do the very best you possibly can, and treat other people like you would like to be treated."
>
> —Coach Lou Holtz

Your Game Plan

What's your game plan? Add the following items to the game plan you are creating for yourself.

- Practice to be positive. Practice to LOOK for the positive and all the great things and happenings that surround us every day.

- Starting today, practice saying "thank you" at least twenty-five times before you have breakfast. You will find that this simple exercise will make you a better person.

- Give whenever possible. Find one opportunity today to give back, whether it be kind words of encouragement, a pat on the back, or something that will help make someone's life a little easier. What goes around comes around.

Chapter Lessons

- There is no such thing as bad inspiration.
- It is up to you to motivate yourself.
- Never let the words of others dictate your future or limit your success.
- Only you decide your own destiny.
- Choose to be positive.
- Think positively.
- Practice saying "thank you."
- It is your time to give.
- What goes around comes around.
- Do what is right, do the very best you possibly can, and treat other people the way you would like to be treated.

COACH RUDY TOMJANOVICH

NBA Player/Coach of the Houston Rockets

Rising Above It All

Coach Rudy T. is one of the great success stories in the NBA. He's a five-time all-star NBA player who went on to be a two-time NBA Championship coach for the Houston Rockets. This is a record few coaches have been able to accomplish. Coach Rudy is a genuine and caring person. I asked him when he knew he wanted to be a coach.

Rudy Tomjanovich

"Believe it or not, I never wanted to be a coach; it was not part of a plan. The basketball part was easy. When I was a kid, I remember I was walking with my family. We came to a school yard and we heard some commotion inside a building. I was five years old and I asked my dad what that noise was. So my father lifted me up on his shoulders and I looked through this window and I saw these guys playing basketball. I remember saying to myself, one of these days I would like to play this game like these big guys were playing."

There was always a "trigger" that went off in the head of the champions we've hear from that said, "One day I want to do that!" Be sure you pay attention to your own triggers. You will get excited about many things in your life. Make sure you pay attention to what your heart is telling you, and please don't discount it. Be true to yourself and listen to your instincts.

Coach Rudy went on to say, "My uncle was a really good mentor for me, my uncle Joe. At a young age he told me the facts of life and my situation. Our family didn't have money and if I wanted to go to college it would have to be on scholarship. He told me I should play a sport and keep my grades up and possibly there could be a future for me. Of course they wanted me to be a baseball player and I was an all-star player. I did that but I didn't love it. I eventually got burnt out and didn't want to play baseball anymore. I went to my uncle and told him that I didn't want to play anymore and he told me that I shouldn't quit and that I should stick with it.

"During a game one day, my uncle witnessed the coach treating me poorly. He told me after the game that he wouldn't want to play for a coach like that either, so I quit. He then asked me what I was going to do. The plan was to do well in a sport and go to college. I told him that I would play basketball. He said, 'Well you were an all star in baseball, there was no reason why you couldn't be an all star in basketball, too.'"

Here is a guy who was talented enough to be an all-star in a sport he didn't really like. That is why it is so vitally important to find something you truly love to do, and you'll never work a day in your life. Rudy had to start over and find a sport that he could be good enough in to receive a scholarship. He goes on to say:

"It's funny, I got on a junior high basketball team but never got into a game. I practiced a lot and I worked hard at the game. My freshman year I was trying out for the team and a buddy of mine saw the list, he came and told me that I didn't make the team. I told him I was as good as any one of them. I went into what would have been my last practice and challenged the biggest guy on the team to a one on one. He was a linebacker and he didn't know much about the game. Every time I dribbled he would treat it like a fumble, so the game became very physical. He physically beat me up but I beat him in the game. So the coach let me on the team. From there I practiced and I played at the playground from morning till night until I got better, essentially until I became not only an all-state player but an all-American player as well."

Perseverance remains the key to any success story.

"In my professional career I had different heroes I looked up to. When I was a player my hero was Dave DeBusschere who played for the New York Knicks. At the age of twenty-four or twenty-five he was the youngest player to ever be a player-coach in the NBA. At the time he was asked by the University of Detroit to come and recruit me. So, this guy who was my hero actually came to my house to pick me up and take me to dinner. That was a really big deal. Later I got a chance to play against the guy. At times I got the better of him, which was really a big deal. How many guys get a chance to play against their idol?"

I asked Coach Rudy about some of the most difficult times in his life. The incredible stories he shared with me showed how much courage he has.

"During my rookie year in the NBA I didn't get a chance to play much, but earlier in the season one of the players got hurt and was going to be out for a month. I went into the game and scored nineteen points and seventeen rebounds. I was excited about the game. The next night I only played a few minutes and the game after that I didn't play at all. I was shocked. I thought

I had a good chance of starting. The coach came to me after the last game and said [that] some players learn from playing and some players learn from watching [and I was] going to have to learn from watching. It was a long year. What I didn't know is the coach was in a war with the general manager and was being forced to bench me because the GM wanted to start another player."

Rudy could have easily listened to the critics, folded up, and quit. Instead, he worked hard to prove them wrong. It is that perseverance that makes him a champion.

Then There Was the Punch

Most certainly, everyone has a time in their life they would like to forget, and "The Punch" is certainly one for Rudy. It's one of sport's infamous stories and, ultimately, it becomes a story of how Rudy was able to forgive.

Despite Rudy's noteworthy career as a player, he is perhaps best remembered for an incident that occurred at the height of his playing career. In a 1977 game, the Los Angeles Lakers' Kermit Washington threw a brutal blindside punch during an on-court melee, which struck Rudy. The blow shattered the bones of his jaw and face and inflicted life-threatening head injuries, leaving him sidelined for five months. He eventually made a full recovery. Although the punch caused much pain, both physical and mental, for Rudy, during his first year back he looked to be the all-star he always was. But after that year his career slowly came to a halt and he was forced to retire in his mid-thirties. Rudy reflects on this experience:

"There was a guy and a very good sports writer named John Feinstein who wanted to write a book on what happened to the guys from the punch. I thought, why bring this thing up, it was long ago and it's over. It was a painful time in my life and it put me out for the entire season. I just got through it and the next year I came back and had a pretty good year; I played one more after that and I retired but I was known for 'The Punch.' Forget about the five all-star teams I made. I was known as the guy who got punched and that was no fun at all. Luckily, later I got into coaching and I changed that whole mentality.

"I believed that if I ever were able to move on, that I had to forgive. Even though I didn't like what he did, I couldn't go around the rest of my life being a victim. I just took myself out of that role and I just said to myself that it was a mistake. And I had to do that because once I get something in my

head and I can't get it out, it just wears me out. I did it to save my own life.
I have learned that having resentment against somebody else creates poison,
and [though] expecting the other person to feel the effect, it's you who feels
the poison, by feeling that negative emotion. So I had to forgive him."

"I believed that if I ever were able to move on, that I had to forgive."
—Coach Rudy Tomjanovich

There are a couple of things to mention here. First, what Rudy does not tell you
is that the punch nearly killed him. Second, to rehab and recover and come
back is a testament to who Rudy really is. Hard work and determination again
prevail. Then, for him to forgive the guy who shortened his career shows
that he's a person of character. Add to that the way Rudy worked to change
people's perception of how he was to be remembered. He refused to be a
victim. He moved on and became one of the most successful NBA coaches.
One of my favorite quotes is one of Coach Rudy's, which I think pretty much
sums up who he is: "Don't ever underestimate the heart of a champion."

Coach Rudy's Message for Students

"First of all you have to have vision of what you want to accomplish. It has to
be something that is believable. It might be hard, might be difficult, but if you
can see it in your mind it will help you achieve it.

"Out of all the things that I did when I was a kid, when I daydreamed and
I had a vision about basketball, it was always a successful action. In my mind I
was successful, I was soaring over other people, I was scoring, rebounding,
and shooting game-winning shots. In the back of my mind that was always
there; I wanted to make that dream come true. However, this is what I believed:
If I value it, then other people will value it too. Know that there isn't going to be
a four-lane highway leading to your ultimate goal. It's going to be a hard climb
up that mountain. To have respect for the journey you are going to take is very
important. Other people want it, they are going to be working hard for it too."

"First of all you have to have vision of what you want to accomplish.
It has to be something that is believable. It might be hard, might be
difficult, but if you can see it in your mind it will help you achieve it."
—Coach Rudy Tomjanovich

"So when I was a kid I used to think that just putting in the time was
enough. My philosophy was, work harder and work longer and you will

beat the other guy. This will help you, you will get better at your skills and conditioning, but a better way is learn the correct way and work on it. Do the right things. Just putting in work isn't going to guarantee success; you have to put in the right work. So you have to find out the right way to do it, the fundamentals, and respect them.

"Because it's hard, there are going to be setbacks. You can use setbacks in different ways."

A Collection of Quotes

"If you have no idea what you are doing, where you are going, or how you're going to get there, you will probably fail."
page xiii

"Your success will be based on your track record and your experience."
page xv

"You choose whether to be successful or not!"
page xvi

"We all have to work like a champion, if we want to become a champion."
page 1

"All champions have one thing in common, the ability to Stick To It!"
page 2

"Champions have the heart of a lion and the will of a warrior."
page 3

"I never considered myself a great player, I had just enough ability to be a good player, and I wanted to be a great player. The desire in me to work my tail off made it happen."
Coach Mike Singletary, San Francisco 49ers
page 3

"Stickability, that's the reason for my success."
Herman Perridan
page 4

"Market your own uniqueness."
Herman Perridan
page 5

"If you just keep working hard, you'll find that people will
believe in you; then there is no limit to what you can obtain."
George Foreman
page 9

"I would rather entertain and hope that people learned something
than educate people and hope they were entertained."
Walt Disney
page 12

"Too many times with today's generation I find that students
are looking for a degree and not an education. This is not
the correct approach."
Dr. Rick Rigsby, Author and nationally acclaimed speaker
page 12

"I could have been a Rhodes Scholar, except for my grades."
Duffy Daugherty, Michigan State
page 13

"We can't solve problems by using the same kind of thinking
we used when we created them."
Albert Einstein
page 13

"There is no one else to blame if you fail."
page 14

"What inspires me every day is what I don't know."
page 18

"No one can make you feel inferior without your consent."
Eleanor Roosevelt
page 19

"Working, volunteering, experiencing, and learning with these
great chefs helped pave my road to success."
page 20

"Imagine how powerful the tool of volunteering is."
page 21

"The power of networking is immeasurable."
page 21

"Give yourself an opportunity to win."
page 21

"Opportunity is missed by most people because it is dressed
in overalls and looks like work."
Thomas Edison
page 26

"You need to start working on establishing an uncompromising
level of work ethic now."
page 26

"If you are fifteen minutes early, you are already
thirty minutes late."
page 29

"Identify fantastic work practices and make them habits."
page 30

"Motivate yourself; don't wait for others to motivate you."
page 32

"That attribute of not being lazy is so admirable.
The world is full of lazy. The world is full
of mediocre."
page 32

"I wanted to learn everything I could about what it takes to be
a great chef. It was a turning point for me."
Thomas Keller
page 34

"Your work ethic should be so incredible, so focused,
so intense that you will never be passed over for
a position or promotion.
You will never be denied."
page 35

"Remember, never to forget, what is your dream, what is your life,
what is your beloved profession."
Bele Karolyi
page 38

"Every day I had to repeat to myself, 'This is not forever.
This is just for survival and . . . I am not going
to die today.' "
Bele Karolyi
page 39

"Spending your life in a profession that you don't like is a
very dull and sad story."
Bela Karolyi
page 39

"WIN: What's Important NOW? "
Lou Holtz
page 42

"NEVER do nothing."
page 43

"When the going gets tough, that's when you need
to get back to the basics."
Chef Sam Choy
page 55

"You can't eat a tomato without planting a seed first."
Chef Sam Choy
page 56

"Keep it simple and bear down."
Chef Sam Choy
page 56

"Just make something happen, that is where
I have been my strongest."
Chef Sam Choy
page 57

"You can't stay in your corner of the forest waiting for
others to come to you. You have to go to them sometimes."
Winnie the Pooh
page 60

"If you want to be an average employee with average
wages and an average lifestyle, just do the minimum."
page 62

"When you're curious, you find lots of interesting
things to do."
Walt Disney
page 63

"Don't think about how you're not getting paid, but how
you're getting ahead."
page 64

"Sometimes you have to pretend to be something
before you can become it."
page 65

"If the person you are talking to doesn't appear to be listening,
be patient. It may simply be that he has a small piece
of fluff in his ear."
Winnie the Pooh
page 66

"I guess what I am trying to say is that I want them to be hungry.
I want them to be successful and eager to learn, but that
greatness and excellence takes time."
Chef Norman Van Aken
page 70

"Students should understand that there are going to be
challenges and setbacks along the way."
Chef Norman Van Aken
page 71

"My advice to young people would be to read. If you read
you are learning . . . "
Chef Norman Van Aken
page 72

"Some people look for success in results that are
tangible. This is not the only place that results
and success show up."
Chef Norman Van Aken
page 74

"I take the high road because I like the view."
Chef Norman Van Aken
page 74

"Lack of a plan + lack of focus = failure!"
page 75

"The road to success is dotted with many tempting parking places."
Author unknown
page 76

"Don't be afraid to give your best to what seemingly are small jobs.
Every time you conquer one it makes you that much stronger.
If you do the little jobs well, the big ones will tend to
take care of themselves."
Dale Carnegie
page 80

"Greatness does not come in a forty-hour work week."
page 80

"I decided if I was going to take the job, that
I was going to make a difference."
Mrs. Joanne Herring
page 84

"The one thing I learned over and over in my life is that
work longer and harder than anybody else you'll win."
Mrs. Joanne Herring
page 85

"Decide what you are going to do and go through it in your
mind and envision your success."
Mrs. Joanne Herring
page 86

"Develop a personal discipline that will set you
apart from all the rest."
page 88

"What this power is I cannot say; all I know is that it exists
and it becomes available only when a man is in that
state of mind in which he knows exactly
what he wants and is fully determined
not to quit until he finds it."
Alexander Graham Bell
page 89

"Promise me you'll never forget me because if I thought you
would I'd never leave."
Winnie the Pooh
page 92

"I remember my roommate in college asking me what
I was going to do after graduation and I told her that I was going
back to Houston and change how people eat."
Chef Monica Pope
page 95

"We decided many years ago that we were going to anchor
ourselves to seasonality, celebration, and hospitality.
I love to cook, I love good food and I love great wine."
Chef Monica Pope
page 95

"That's how I have been trained my whole life, that you
put your head down and swim to the other side of the pool
and get there as fast as you can."
Chef Monica Pope
page 95

"Just do good work. There is good food and then
there is great food and then there is meaningful food.
Ask yourself, 'Who are you, what are you, and
what are you really about?'"
Chef Monica Pope
page 96

"I hire on the heart and rarely on the resume."
page 98

"We receive three educations, one from our parents,
one from our schoolmasters, and one from the world. The third
contradicts all that the first two teach us."
Charles Louis de Secondat, Baron de Montesquieu
page 98

"Success seems to be largely a matter of hanging on
after others have let go."
William Feather
page 99

"Difficult things take a long time, impossible things a little longer."
Author unknown
page 100

"If you at first are denied for the position, be
comfortably persistent."
page 100

"I have been up against tough competition all my life.
I wouldn't know how to get along without it."
Walt Disney
page 101

"I tried to become a complete player and emulate
the guys [who] were so great."
Charlie Frazier
page 104

"I worked hard in my life and after I made the team
I wanted to be sure I stayed on the team."
Charlie Frazier
page 106

"Speed was my weapon so I had to be sure
I was the best I could be."
Charlie Frazier
page 106

"You have to write the script and plan the ending yourself."
page 108

"Sometimes we are not searching for inspiration,
but inspiration finds us."
page 109

"Don't ever let the words of others dictate your future
or limit your success."
Chef Clark Bernier
page 110

"So don't stop "looking"! Keep looking for the good, and
you will find it."
page 113

"You choose if you're going to be successful or not, nobody else."
page 116

"Once you have grown into a great chef, it is your
duty to give back."
page 117

"I believed that if I ever were able to move on,
that I had to forgive."
Coach Rudy Tomjanovich
page 123

"Don't ever underestimate the heart of a champion."
Coach Rudy Tomjanovich
page 123

"First of all you have to have vision of what you want to accomplish.
It has to be something that is believable. It might be hard,
might be difficult, but if you can see it in your mind
it will help you achieve it."
Coach Rudy Tomjanovich
page 123

Index